D1052987

# WOODROW WILSON

## AND THE

# PROGRESSIVE ERA

# WOODROW WILSON

## AND THE
# PROGRESSIVE ERA

Bonnie L. Lukes

## MORGAN REYNOLDS
### PUBLISHING
Greensboro, North Carolina

# WORLD LEADERS

GEORGE C. MARSHALL
ADOLF HITLER
WOODROW WILSON
VACLAV HAVEL
GENGHIS KHAN
JOSEPH STALIN
CHE GUEVARA

WOODROW WILSON AND THE PROGRESSIVE ERA

Copyright © 2006 by Bonnie L. Lukes

Library of Congress Cataloging-in-Publication Data

Lukes, Bonnie L.
    Woodrow Wilson and the Progressive Era / Bonnie L. Lukes.— 1st ed.
    p. cm.
    Includes bibliographical references and index.
    ISBN-13: 978-1-931798-79-2 (library binding)
    ISBN-10: 1-931798-79-6 (library binding)
1. Wilson, Woodrow, 1856-1924—Juvenile literature. 2. Presidents—United
States—Biography—Juvenile literature. 3. United States—Politics and
government—1913-1921—Juvenile literature. I. Title.
    E767.L95 2005
    917.913—dc22
                                    2005015999

Printed in the United States of America
First Edition

*To my daughters Kelly and Sandi,*
*who validate my life*

# CONTENTS

# EARLY YEARS

## ≈ ONE ≈

Tommy Wilson did not learn the alphabet until he was nine years old. He did not read well until age eleven and remained a slow reader all his life. In school, he daydreamed, and his grades suffered as a result. He was accused of laziness. Relatives whispered that he was slow, incapable of learning. Though he would continue to struggle academically, Tommy Wilson would eventually obtain a law degree and a PhD, showing the courage and determination that would help him achieve the highest office in the land.

Thomas Woodrow Wilson was born on December 28, 1856—almost five years before America was torn apart by civil war. Called Tommy as a boy, he was the first son and third child of Joseph Ruggles Wilson and Janet

*Opposite:* Thomas Woodrow Wilson. *(Library of Congress)*

Woodrow Wilson's parents, Joseph Ruggles Wilson and Janet "Jessie" Wilson. *(Princeton University Library)*

"Jessie" Woodrow Wilson. The couple, descendents of hardscrabble Scotch-Irish immigrants and devoted members of the Presbyterian faith, had met and married in Steubenville, Ohio. Soon after, Joseph accepted a teaching position at Hampden-Sydney College in Virginia.

Joseph Wilson was an outgoing, cheerful man with a brilliant mind and a quick wit. Moving from the Midwest to the South meant adjusting to a different culture, but neither Joseph nor Jessie had any difficulty with the

The town of Staunton, Virginia, where Woodrow Wilson was born on December 28, 1856. *(Library of Congress)*

change. They both loved the South, and Joseph would spend the remainder of his professional life there. He saw no conflict between the institution of slavery and his Christian faith. When the Civil War began, he supported the Confederacy.

The Wilsons welcomed the births of two daughters, Anne and Marion, while at Hampden-Sydney. In 1854, Joseph moved the family to nearby Staunton, Virginia, to begin a career as a pastor. The future president was born there, but before he was two years old, the family moved again, this time to Augusta, Georgia.

Reverend Wilson's church in Augusta covered nearly an entire block. Its affluent congregation built the family a new redbrick parsonage just across the street from the church. Woodrow Wilson said that his earliest memory

The Wilsons' brick house in Augusta still stands amidst the city's downtown today.
*(Library of Congress)*

was of standing at the entrance to that house when he was four years old and hearing a passerby say, "Mr. Lincoln was elected and there [is] to be war." He had to ask his father what that meant.

The Civil War began a few months later, and Augusta became a haven for refugees from besieged cities like Savannah. Reverend Wilson turned his church into a hospital for the wounded and the churchyard into a prison stockade for Union soldiers. Tommy would remember little about the war itself, but he would not escape its aftermath.

The Civil War left the country bitter and divided. The terrain of the South had been devastated. Cities like Atlanta, Columbia, and Richmond had been burned. The economy was in ruins. Financial institutions were bankrupt. Federal troops occupied the cities.

Although the Wilsons' social status and comfortable financial position shielded Tommy to some degree, the chaos and disunity all around him left a deep impression. These youthful experiences may account for his lifelong efforts to create a state of harmony and unity in everything from baseball teams to nations.

Tommy was eight years old when the war ended. At that time he began his formal education at a private school for boys run by Joseph T. Derry, a former officer in the Confederate Army. For Tommy, it was the beginning of a long struggle. He could not master reading, and his grades were below average. He appeared to be uninterested in learning. It is now generally accepted that he probably suffered from dyslexia, a learning disorder that interferes with a person's ability to read.

Tommy much preferred games to schooling. He and his friends organized a baseball team they called the Lightfoot Club. Tommy was not the best player, but his teammates apparently recognized his leadership qualities because they elected him club president. The Lightfoots held meetings in the Wilsons' barn, and Tommy eventually made up a set of rules to help settle arguments.

Young Tommy had a strong sense of responsibility. He often rode his horse to visit his favorite cousin, Jessie Bones. They both relished James Fenimore Cooper's stories of wilderness adventure, and playing in the woods near Jessie's house. One day, Jessie was pretending to be a squirrel in a tree while Tommy played the part of the hunter, and he shot her with his toy bow and arrow.

He was horrified when Jessie fell out of the tree and landed unconscious at his feet. He carried her back to the house where he bravely confessed, "I am a murderer. It wasn't an accident. I killed her." Fortunately, Jessie recovered unharmed.

The year Tommy turned fourteen his father accepted a professorship at the Columbia Theological Seminary in Columbia, South Carolina. This meant uprooting the family, which now included four children. A second son, Joseph, had been born when Tommy was ten.

Unlike Augusta, Columbia had not escaped the Civil War unscathed. Everything in the town—except for the capitol building and the churches—had been burned to the ground. In 1870, the year the Wilsons arrived, it remained a wasteland. Seeing the destructive results of combat made a lasting impression on Tommy, one that

When General William Tecumseh Sherman's army passed through Columbia at the close of the Civil War, much of the city was destroyed by fire and looting. It would take decades for the city to recover. *(Library of Congress)*

would influence his future attitude toward war.

In Columbia, Tommy continued his schooling with Professor Charles Barnwell, who held classes in a barn near the seminary. Tommy still struggled with certain subjects—especially math—but he had finally learned to read, and his powers of concentration had improved. He enjoyed reading sea stories and daydreaming about swashbuckling adventures.

When Tommy was fifteen, he read in *Boys and Girls Weekly* about a shorthand method of taking notes. He set out to teach himself the system. This required great effort and determination, but he succeeded. For the rest of his life he used shorthand to make entries in his diary and prepare first drafts of speeches or articles. "To save time is to lengthen life," he wrote in his shorthand notebook. That may have been his only reason for learning shorthand, but perhaps he also enjoyed that it was a kind of secret code. It is also possible that he instinctively used shorthand as a way to overcome his dyslexia.

In the summer of 1873, when Tommy was sixteen, he formally joined the Presbyterian Church. Throughout his life, he never questioned his religious faith. He might have disagreed with some of the church's conservative views—as he did when his uncle was fired for preaching evolution—but he never doubted its fundamental teachings. Wherever he was, in whatever circumstances, he prayed daily and read his Bible. "I do not see how any one can sustain himself in any enterprise in life without prayer," he once wrote.

By fall of 1873, Tommy's grades had improved enough for him to enroll at Davidson College, a Presbyterian school near Charlotte, North Carolina. His father served on the school's board of trustees. Davidson was primarily a school for training young men interested in entering the ministry, and Tommy's parents may have picked the school because they hoped he would follow in his father's footsteps. However, there is no indication that he seriously considered becoming a pastor.

At Davidson, he was one of 107 students. He joined a debating club and played center field for the baseball team. His grades were average, as were his baseball skills. The captain of his team once said, "Tommy Wilson would be a good player if he weren't so damned lazy!" Overall, his year at Davidson was satisfactory, and he looked forward to returning in September. But he never went back. Wilson said later it was because of poor health. He may, however, have succumbed to pressure from his mother, who wanted him nearby. In any case, he returned home to Columbia just months before his father moved the family to Wilmington, North Carolina.

Wilson spent fifteen months out of school. It was a lonely time. He missed his friends at Davidson. The only upside was that Wilmington was a port city, and he was still fascinated by the sea. He filled the empty hours hanging around the docks, enjoying the bustle of activities, and talking to the sailors. For a time he even considered enrolling in the Naval Academy. When Wilson wasn't at the dock, he worked on perfecting his shorthand technique, and he now read extensively—especially books on history and politics.

Wilson found little intellectual stimulation in Wilmington, but the exception was John Bellamy, who later would be elected to Congress. They both enjoyed reading historical novels, and this common interest led to a lasting friendship. Wilson might have made other friends if he had reached out more. But emotionally he was shy and turned in on himself. Physically, he had grown rapidly in a short time and was not yet comfortable with the change, which made him feel gawky and awkward.

At some point in this frustrating period, Wilson decided to enroll at the College of New Jersey at Princeton—later called Princeton University. The president of Princeton may have influenced this decision when he visited the Wilson home in December 1874 and told the family that Tommy "seemed to be good college material." That Princeton was a Presbyterian college, and tuition was free for the son of a

Despite Wilson's rocky relationship with formal education, he would eventually find an apt home at the College of New Jersey at Princeton. *(Library of Congress)*

Presbyterian minister, offered additional incentive.

Wilson, nearly nineteen, left for Princeton in the fall of 1875. It was a tough adjustment. Not only was he a southerner in a northern college, which set him apart, but he was forced to live off campus because no rooms were available. This isolated him from school activities. He was also still somewhat shy and withdrawn. However, before the year ended, he and other students living at his boarding house formed a baseball team called the Bowery Boys. They played frequent games against similar teams, sometimes two a day. By the end of his freshman year, he was taking an active part in college life.

His second year began what Wilson described in his diary as the "magical years" that would transform a shy, awkward boy into a confident young man. The transformation began when he moved into Witherspoon, a newly completed dormitory on campus. There he met a group of young men who shared his intellectual interests. He would learn almost as much from these new friends as he did from his professors. They called themselves the Witherspoon gang. Charles Talcott, who became one of Wilson's closest friends, was made president of the gang, and Wilson its secretary of state.

Wilson also became managing editor of the *Princetonian,* the university newspaper. He was growing increasingly interested in government and politics. He and Charles Talcott made a pact in which they pledged to "acquire knowledge that we might have power . . . in leading others into our ways of thinking." Already anticipating a career in politics, Wilson even wrote out cards inscribed "Thomas Woodrow Wilson, Senator from Virginia" to see how that looked and sounded. He worked on his oratory skills until he developed an easygoing, conversational style in his speeches.

Meanwhile, he did not neglect sports. He became president of the baseball association and mastered the

A class picture of Wilson while he was attending Princeton. *(Library of Congress)*

rules of football, a new sport on campus. About team sports, he said, *"Everything* depends upon the character of the captain and president [of the team]. . . . The president must, above all things else, be a man of unbiased judgment, energy, determination, intelligence, moral courage, *conscience."* All his life he would judge leaders—especially himself—by this standard.

In his sophomore year, Wilson became interested in British history. On his own, he read multiple histories of the English people and studied the speeches of British statesmen like Edmond Burke. He especially admired British prime minister William Gladstone, the great orator and reformer who had founded his political career upon strong religious principles.

This high regard for the British political system influenced Wilson's early political views. In his senior year, he wrote an essay entitled "Cabinet Government in the United States," in which he suggested that Congress and the president be replaced by a parliamentary government similar to the system used in England. This was not a new idea, but Wilson expressed it in such clear and reasoned language that it was accepted for publication in the renowned *International Review,* a widely read journal.

Publication in the *International Review* was a major accomplishment for one so young, and it reinforced Wilson's ambitions. When he graduated Princeton in June 1879, he was twenty-three years old and confident that his future lay in politics.

# FINDING A PATH

## ⪻ TWO ⪼

In the fall of 1879, Wilson entered the University of Virginia to study law. "The profession I chose was politics," he wrote later, "[but] the profession I entered was the law. I entered the one because I thought it would lead to the other."

Studying law, however, proved dull and wearisome. The philosophy of law intrigued Wilson, but he detested the countless petty details. "I wish . . . to record the confession that I am most terribly bored by the noble study of Law," he wrote to his old Princeton friend Charles Talcott.

At first he was lonely, missing the camaraderie of friends like Talcott. But in October he joined the Phi Kappa Psi fraternity, where he developed new friendships. His closest fraternity friend was Heath Dabney,

The stately campus of the University of Virginia, where Wilson attended law school. *(Library of Congress)*

who found Wilson "full of fun and tomfoolery." They shared private jokes and gave each other silly, affectionate nicknames like "thou illimitable idiot." The friendship—and the nicknames—would endure throughout their lives.

Wilson also joined a debating club and was soon appointed its recording secretary. He always signed the minutes "T. Woodrow Wilson," and before long, preferring the simpler Woodrow Wilson, he dropped even the "T." Friends, however, continued to call him Tommy.

This marked a period of intense activity for Wilson. In addition to fraternity duties (in his second year, he was elected Phi Kappa Psi's president) and public debates, he contributed articles to both the university newspaper and the school's literary magazine. He also joined the glee club, partly because its major purpose was to serenade girls. Describing a night when the club was out until one o'clock serenading girls in town, Wilson wrote that they had "a very jolly, amusing time, listening to the tittering at the windows, and collecting in the dark the flowers that were thrown to us."

Unfortunately, such a demanding schedule eventually took a toll physically. In December 1880, just six months shy of completing the two-year course of study, illness forced Wilson to drop out of law school. He was disgusted. "How can a man with a weak body ever arrive anywhere?" he asked. The exact nature of his illness is vague, but emotional factors may have played a part. He had fallen in love with his cousin, Hattie Woodrow, who lived near the university. At one point, he cut so many of his classes to visit her that he was reprimanded by school officials.

Back in Wilmington, Wilson studied law on his own. By the summer of 1882, he had completed his studies and regained his health. He planned to start practicing law by the end of the year. In the meantime, he visited relatives in Ohio, mostly because Hattie was there. During the visit, Wilson asked her to marry him. She turned him down. He thought she refused him because she did not believe in marriage between first cousins. But the truth was that Hattie loved someone else.

Stunned by this rejection, Wilson moped around, drifting aimlessly through the winter, doing little more than writing bad poetry. Finally, in May 1882, he moved to Atlanta, Georgia, and set up a law office with Edward Renick, a friend from the University of Virginia.

Wilson did not enjoy practicing law any more than he had liked studying it. "The philosophical study of the law . . . is a very different matter from its scheming and haggling practice," he wrote Dabney. When he complained in letters to his family, his father urged him to persevere. But by the end of April 1883, after less than a year in practice, Woodrow had decided that his future lay in teaching and writing. He applied for a fellowship at Johns Hopkins University in Baltimore, Maryland.

"My purpose in coming to the university is to qualify myself for teaching . . . history and political science," he wrote on his admission application. He did not receive the fellowship but enrolled anyway. Now twenty-seven, he was once again dependent on his father for financial support.

Before the fall term could begin in September, something else changed in Wilson's life. In the spring, he had traveled to Rome, Georgia, on business for his mother. He attended Sunday services at Rome's Presbyterian church, and it was there he first saw Ellen Axson. One look at her "bright, pretty face," her "splendid, laughing eyes," and Woodrow fell hopelessly in love.

Learning that Ellen was the minister's daughter, he wasted no time in calling on her. The visit—made that same afternoon—did not go as he envisioned it. Reverend Axson thought the young man had come to see him. He looked surprised when Wilson asked about his daughter, but he called her into his study and introduced them. They could do little more than say hello because Reverend Axson wanted to discuss problems in the church. Wilson tried to respond appropriately, but he could not keep his eyes and thoughts away from Ellen.

He did not let this awkward first meeting deter him.

Ellen Louise Axson as she looked around the time when she first met Wilson.
*(Princeton University Library)*

He sent a note asking Ellen to accompany him on an afternoon drive, and she accepted. He had to return to Atlanta, but by May he was back in Rome for a visit.

Ellen Axson would not be easily won. She was twenty-three years old, well-read, and a talented artist. She had studied at Rome Female College in Rome, Georgia, where she had also taken postgraduate classes. Ellen had become educated, Wilson wrote his Princeton friend Robert Bridges, "without knowing it, and without losing one particle of freshness or natural feminine charm."

When Ellen was twenty-one, her mother had died in childbirth. The younger children (including the newborn) had been distributed among relatives, but Ellen felt responsible for them. Since her mother's death, she had run the parsonage and cared for her father, whose health was fragile. Deciding she could never inflict these burdens on anyone else, she had vowed never to marry. That vow, however, was made before she came up against the iron will of Woodrow Wilson. He was not one to give up easily. "I've made up my mind to win her if I can," he wrote Bridges.

Throughout the summer, letters flew back and forth between Woodrow and Ellen, but they did not see each other. Then, on September 14, fate took a hand. Wilson was on his way to Baltimore to begin his first year at Johns Hopkins. He stopped at Asheville, North Carolina, to conduct some business. Ellen happened to be in Asheville visiting a friend. Woodrow was walking down the street when he spotted her in a hotel restaurant. It was a joyous reunion. For three days, they spent every spare moment together. On the third day, Woodrow proposed marriage, and Ellen, forgetting her earlier concerns, said yes.

The newly engaged couple had to part almost immediately. Ellen returned to Rome, Georgia, to care for her
now seriously ill father, and Woodrow continued on to
Johns Hopkins for the start of the fall term. He wrote her
later that he had been unable to take it in that she had
agreed to marry him: "I remember being . . . utterly
unable to speak . . . of the love and joy that were in my
heart." Following his initial euphoria, however, it hit him
that he had a year or more at Johns Hopkins before he
could secure a professorship and earn enough to support
them. They could not marry until then. It seemed an
eternity to the love-struck Wilson, but he found a rooming house in the heart of Baltimore and resigned himself
to the wait.

To Wilson, giving up law to enter the academic world
meant abandoning his lifelong dream of a career in
politics. "Professors," he reminded Ellen, "could not
participate actively in political affairs." He insisted,
however, that "the occupancy of office had never been
an important part of his political plan" anyway. Instead,
he could be an "*outside* force in politics" through his
writing.

His goal, he told Ellen, was "to contribute to our
literature what no American has ever contributed, studies in the philosophy of our institutions . . . I want to . . .
present their weakness and their strength . . . with such skill
. . . that it shall be seen . . . that I have added something
to the resources of knowledge upon which statecraft
must depend." Nevertheless, he admitted that he felt a

"lurking sense of . . . *loss,* as if I had missed . . . something upon which both my gifts and inclinations gave me a claim."

In his first month at Hopkins, Wilson was disappointed by the required courses. "I have no patience," he wrote Ellen, "for the tedious toil of what is known as 'research.'" He went to see Herbert Baxter Adams, who headed the Hopkins Department of History and Politics. He explained his frustration with the program and expounded on his personal interest in the history of constitutional government. Then, with what was either supreme self-confidence or full-blown egotism, he requested that he be permitted to explore this topic in his own way (which today would be called independent

Wilson moved to the port city of Baltimore in 1883 to attend Johns Hopkins University. *(Library of Congress)*

Always drawn to campus activities, Wilson *(back row, second from left)* is pictured here with the glee club he helped to found at Johns Hopkins. *(Johns Hopkins University)*

study). Adams, who apparently recognized that he was dealing with an unusual student, granted the request.

Able to follow his own path, Wilson began to enjoy the university. He joined a debating club and soon became a leader in campus activities. He wrote a new constitution for the debating club and helped found the Johns Hopkins Glee Club. He was content, and much of that contentment revolved around Ellen. On September 25, just a week after their parting, he had sent her an engagement ring. In a declaration that revealed a keen understanding of his own personality, he wrote, "I suppose there never was a man more dependent than I on love and sympathy, more devoted to home and home life. . . .

I shall not begin to live a complete life, my love, until you are my wife." Wilson's long-jawed face and steely eyes gazing through pince-nez glasses gave the impression of an aloof, unresponsive individual. But this stiff demeanor concealed a passionate nature that was revealed in his letters to Ellen. "I am at a loss to know how to express myself," he wrote in one letter, "[because] my inclination is to be 'making love' in every sentence." And in another: "Thoughts of you fill my life. You seem to be in everything I read, in everything I do."

Ellen, meanwhile, was caring for her father, who was physically ill and suffering from depression. She and Woodrow would have to spend the Christmas holidays apart. Wilson, alone in his deserted Baltimore rooming house, tried to keep busy. On New Year's Day, 1884, he sat down at a desk and began writing the first of a series of essays analyzing the American political system.

Early in the new year, Ellen's father became violent, and she had to commit him to the Georgia State Mental Hospital. His health did not improve, and in May he took his own life. Ellen was devastated. Wilson, feeling helpless so far away, wanted to skip his second year at Johns Hopkins and take a job so they could be married immediately. Ellen insisted he continue his studies.

Wilson went home to Wilmington for the summer and completed the political essays, which he now hoped to publish in book form. He wanted Ellen to meet his parents, and in September she came to visit. After enjoying three weeks together, they boarded the same train, headed for separate destinations. He returned to Baltimore to begin his second year at Johns Hopkins, and she went to New York to enroll at the Art Students League. She was now twenty-five and he was twenty-eight.

Wilson wanted to get married as soon as he finished at Johns Hopkins and pressed Ellen to set a wedding date. But she hesitated. She had already achieved some acclaim as an artist, and now, at the league, she was mastering new techniques and enjoying the school's free and easy atmosphere. Having cared for her father for so long, it was a relief to be able to relax and attend only to her own needs.

Wilson found this difficult to understand. Like many men of the time, he saw women as fragile and needing protection. In turn they were expected to devote themselves to the men in their lives. That Ellen might consider a career in art over marriage was a foreign idea to him. "Women . . . have mental and moral gifts of a sort . . . that men lack . . . but their life must *supplement* man's life," he told Ellen. He never completely overcame these feelings, but with Ellen's gentle tutoring, he did ultimately understand what she sacrificed to marry him. "It hurts me," he wrote her before their wedding, ". . . to think that I am asking you to give up what has formed so much of your life."

Soon after returning to Johns Hopkins in September, Wilson sent his completed manuscript off to Houghton-Mifflin, a leading publisher of the day. Six weeks went by with no word. Then everything seemed to happen at once.

On November 27, 1884, he wrote Ellen that he had an interview with the trustees of a newly founded woman's college at Bryn Mawr, Pennsylvania—just outside Philadelphia. They were interested in Wilson for their history department. "I should certainly accept any offer from them that included salary enough for us to live on," he wrote Ellen. But first he wanted to know how she felt about it.

Ellen understood her future husband well. The dean of Bryn Mawr was a woman, and Ellen questioned whether he could handle that. "I fear you would find it very unpleasant to serve . . . under a *woman*," she wrote

Bryn Mawr's female dean, the formidable Carey Thomas.

back. She assured him, however, that she would be happy with whatever he decided.

In the same mail, Wilson received a letter from Houghton-Mifflin saying they wanted to publish his book. Jubilant, he wrote to Ellen, "They have actually offered me as good terms as if I were already a well-known writer! The success . . . almost takes my breath away. . . . Your love makes this first success sweet; because you share it." The book, which would be titled *Congressional Government,* expanded on the theme of his first article, "Cabinet Government in the United States." It argued that Congress had become the most powerful branch of the government, overshadowing even the executive branch, and explained clearly and concisely how Congress functioned.

As the Christmas holidays approached, Wilson waited to hear from Bryn Mawr. Determined not to spend another Christmas apart from Ellen, he went to New York and rented a room near her residence. During their eight days together, they decided he should accept the Bryn Mawr position if the terms were right.

Back in Baltimore on January 13, 1885, he wrote Ellen: "I have heard from Bryn Mawr, little lady! I have been elected 'Associate' in History for two years at $1500 a year." The salary was less than he had hoped, but he admitted that because of his inexperience, it was as much as he would have been offered at any other institution. Did Ellen approve? And if so, he pleaded, "Won't you be thinking of ways to make our marriage possible in June?"

Ellen surrendered and agreed to a June wedding. Wilson was ecstatic. "*Can* it be true that I am to have . . . the loving wife for whom my life has so long waited? . . . Yes, you have promised!"

On June 24, 1885, they were married in the parsonage

of the Independent Presbyterian Church of Savannah. Ellen's grandfather and Woodrow's father performed the ceremony.

"There surely never lived a man with whom love was a more critical matter than it is with me," Wilson had said. That he found this love with Ellen Axson was nothing short of serendipity. And he knew it. She would be the single most important influence in determining his future. With her by his side, he was ready to fulfill his "longing to do immortal work."

# THE PROFESSOR

## ⌒ THREE ⌒

In mid-September 1885, the newlyweds arrived at Bryn Mawr and Wilson began his teaching career. Ellen was two months pregnant. They lived on the upper floor in one of three faculty cottages at the edge of the campus. The cottages lacked adequate heating, and kerosene lamps provided the only lighting. The living quarters were small, allowing little privacy. Nonetheless, Wilson wrote Heath Dabney that he was happier than he had ever been. "I was desperately in need of such a companion as Mrs. W.," he wrote. "I needed to be absorbed by somebody else and I am."

Bryn Mawr was not the first women's college in America, but it was the first to offer a graduate degree. Educating women had only begun to be accepted after the Civil War, and even then their education was prima-

Bryn Mawr as it looked in 1885, its opening year. *(Library of Congress)*

rily limited to learning traditional skills such as home-making. Colleges like Bryn Mawr evolved in order to provide women with a curriculum equal to that offered men.

Wilson, like the majority of men and even many women at that time, did not yet accept that women were intellectually equal to men. He admitted to Ellen that he would "a *great* deal rather teach *men anywhere* . . . than girls at Bryn Mawr." Nevertheless, he settled in to make the best of it. The school was so small that he sometimes had only one or two students in a class. But he prepared his lectures as carefully and thoughtfully as he would have done for a class of thirty.

Ellen suffered from severe nausea and anxiety throughout her pregnancy, and it was decided that she would go to her Aunt Louisa's in Gainesville, Georgia, when it came time for the baby to be born. The baby, a girl, was born on April 16, 1886, and Ellen wrote her husband, "Ah, Sweetheart, it seemed impossible for anything else to bring us closer than we were, but what a wonderful bond of union is this precious little life!"

She worried, though, that he would be disappointed because the baby was not a boy. He immediately reassured her. "I *know* that no [little] 'Woodrow' . . . [could] ever take the place of that dear little girl . . . especially if she be like you!"

Ellen and the baby, who was christened Margaret, would remain in Gainesville until the summer. It was a long separation for the couple, but Woodrow had little time to dwell on his loneliness because he was studying for his PhD. Earlier, as a student at Johns Hopkins, he had decided against acquiring an advanced degree. Now he and Ellen believed this additional credential would help him acquire a position at a larger, more prestigious college. During the last two weeks in May, he made daily trips to Johns Hopkins to take the written and oral exams. Finally, on May 29, he wrote triumphantly to Ellen, "*My own precious little wife,* Hurrah—a thousand times hurrah—I'm through. . . . The degree is actually secured! Oh, the relief of it!"

In June, he sped to Gainesville to reunite with Ellen and meet his daughter. The little family then spent most of their summer vacation with Wilson's parents before returning to Bryn Mawr to begin a new school year.

As Ellen had anticipated, Woodrow grew increasingly dissatisfied with teaching at a women's college. He always displayed a respectful, even chivalrous attitude toward his students, but he could not see the point of teaching political science to women. "Lecturing to young women . . . on the history and principles of politics," he complained, was "about as appropriate" as "lecturing to stone-masons on the evolution of fashion in dress."

He knew women were capable of learning, but he could not envision that any woman could ever play an active role in politics. His ultimate objective was to influence political thinking and shape public affairs, and since, in his opinion, women would never be in government, he thought his time spent teaching them was wasted.

Wilson's discontent at Bryn Mawr was tempered somewhat by the success of *Congressional Government.* Scholars praised the book's clear political thinking and succinct writing style. Periodicals invited him to submit articles. A new publication, *Political Science Quarterly,* asked him to become a regular contributor. Cornell University invited him to speak. This recognition stimulated him to begin writing *The State,* a college textbook on comparative government.

*The State* compared the American system of government with European governments and explained how governments throughout history had worked. In this book, Wilson no longer advocated an American parliament. Instead he proposed ways the existing government could be reformed and made better. *The State* contained the seeds of Wilson's liberalism. For example, he proposed certain reforms to correct social injustices brought about by rapid industrial growth. He supported a ban on child labor and overall improvements in working conditions. However, *The State* did not advocate radical action to bring about reform. "The method of political development," he wrote, "is conservative adaptation . . . modifying old means to accomplish new ends."

He worked on the manuscript in his spare time. Research was a struggle because most of the sources on comparative government were in German, and Wilson—perhaps because of his dyslexia—had always struggled with foreign languages. For a time, he considered resigning and taking his family to Berlin, where he could better learn the German language. But that idea had to be discarded when Ellen became pregnant for the second time.

On August 28, 1887, a second daughter, Jessie Woodrow Wilson, was born. With her birth, the family outgrew their small quarters. Fortunately, that fall Woodrow was promoted to a full professorship, which brought an increase in his pay. They rented an eleven-room house just a block away from the campus. Wilson's mother questioned what they could possibly "want with *eleven* rooms."

Ellen planned to bring her younger brother Eddie,

now eleven, to live with them. (Her other brother Stockton was attending college in the South.) She also invited her cousin Mary Hoyt to live with them so she could attend Bryn Mawr. This marked the beginning of a twenty-year period during which Woodrow and Ellen welcomed numerous young relatives into their home and helped them through school. Ellen's brother Eddie became like a son to both of them.

Despite his promotion, Wilson was unhappy with the slow progress of his career. "Thirty-one years old and nothing done!" he wrote at the beginning of his third year at Bryn Mawr. His salary was still low compared to full professors at other schools, but in February 1888, he had an opportunity to supplement it. Johns Hopkins asked him to give a series of twenty-five guest lectures to its graduate students, for which he would be paid $500. He gladly accepted the offer, welcoming the extra money.

Wilson's growing apprehension that life was passing him by had been intensified by his mother's death the previous April. He wrote to Heath Dabney and described the unexpected vulnerability he felt at her death: "Her loss has left me with a sad, oppressive sense of having somehow *suddenly lost my youth.* I feel old and responsibility-ridden."

In June 1888, he submitted his resignation to Bryn Mawr and accepted a position as professor of history and political economy at Wesleyan University in Middletown, Connecticut. He received a substantial

The pastoral campus of Wesleyan University in Middletown, Connecticut, where Wilson spent two years as a professor. *(Library of Congress)*

increase in pay and would be allowed a six-week leave of absence each year to continue his Johns Hopkins lectures. Of equal importance to Wilson was that he would now be teaching men. "I have for a long time been hungry for a class of *men,*" he wrote Dabney.

Even as Wilson accepted the position at Wesleyan, he knew it was only temporary. His long-term goal was to teach at Princeton, his alma mater. Friends at Princeton were already working behind the scenes to bring that about. Until such time, though, Wilson enjoyed himself at Wesleyan. He made new friends among the faculty, and the Wesleyan students liked and respected him. "I can see him now," one student later recalled, "with his hands forward, the tips of his fingers just touching the table, his face earnest and animated . . . illustrating an otherwise dry and tedious subject by his beautiful language and his apt way of putting things."

Wilson also sponsored a debating team and even helped coach the football team. In 1889, when Wesleyan

Wilson was well liked by his students and colleagues during his short tenure at Wesleyan. He is pictured here *(front row, third from left)* with fellow faculty in 1889. *(AP Photo)*

had a winning record, the students acknowledged Wilson's enthusiastic support by serenading him at his home.

At Wesleyan he had more time for writing, and he soon completed the manuscript for *The State*. He wrote Ellen from one of his lecture trips that he had acquired a sense of maturity, "the feeling that I need no longer hesitate . . . to assert myself . . . in the presence of 'my elders.'" *The State* was published in the fall, making its debut at the same time the Wilsons' third daughter, Eleanor, made hers.

The following summer, Wilson—who for several years had devoted summer vacations to work—spent a week in New York with his friend Robert Bridges. They visited Coney Island, and Wilson saw his first professional baseball game. He also lunched with Dr. Francis Patton, the recently elected president of Princeton. Dr. Patton offered him a professorship in the economics department, but Wilson refused the offer. He did not want to teach economics; he wanted to teach politics. He also felt an obligation to the Wesleyan trustees, who were expecting him to stay for at least two years.

Wilson's reputation was bolstered by *The State's* excellent reviews. One of its merits was that it made available in English much information that had previously been accessible only to advanced scholars. Harvard University was quick to adopt it as a textbook. As a result, Albert Bushnell Hart, a Harvard professor who was editing a three-book series on American history, asked Wilson to write the final installment. It would cover the years from Andrew Jackson's presidency through the Civil War and Reconstruction. Wilson's father worried that as a southerner, his son's book would show bias toward the South, but Woodrow was equally certain that he had moved beyond regional prejudices.

In the summer of 1889, Wilson set to work on the book, which he would title *Division and Reunion*. His premise would be that the Civil War was a result of the economical and social differences between the North and South. He also held that slavery was economically wasteful and that the South was better off without it.

He was still working on the book in February when a second offer came from Princeton, and this time he felt comfortable accepting. A professorship at Princeton had been Wilson's goal for four years, and now, at age thirty-four, he looked forward to new challenges. He knew he was starting down a different road, but even in his wildest imaginings he could not have anticipated how far it would take him.

# REACHING THE EMERALD CITY

## ⌒ FOUR ⌒

In 1890, the village of Princeton existed much the same as it had when Wilson lived there as a student fifteen years earlier. At the college, however, enrollment had almost doubled, and other changes were evident as well. In Wilson's era, students dressed in suits and ties; now the accepted dress was casual: corduroy trousers and turtleneck sweaters. Athletic events took precedence over debating clubs. As in colleges all across the country, educators now placed less emphasis on the theological and classical and more on modern history and science.

Dr. Francis Patton, the president of Princeton, was a Presbyterian minister conservative in nature and slow to make changes. He had hired Wilson not only because he thought his youth and brilliance would bring new en-

Princeton president Dr. Francis Patton. *(Princeton University Library)*

ergy to Princeton, but also because he saw him as a fellow conservative who valued tradition. As others would do in the future, Dr. Patton underestimated Wilson's drive and determination. Wilson had put aside his dream of holding public office, but he retained his resolve to influence the thoughts and actions of others. He had definite ideas about how Princeton must change in order to become "the perfect place of learning."

Wilson was popular with Princeton students. His informal, clear, and vibrant lectures made his class in public law the most sought after on campus, and year after year students voted him their favorite professor. He

Wilson as a professor at Princeton University. *(Library of Congress)*

was one of the few faculty members involved with extracurricular campus activities. Occasionally he acted as an intermediary between faculty and students. One year, during a performance staged for the faculty, the seniors performed a song they had written that ridiculed certain unpopular teachers. Some professors wanted to forbid the song, but Wilson convinced them it would be impossible to do and that it would only make them look ridiculous to try.

As a result, the students added a new verse:

> Here's to Woodrow Wilson, oh,
> Our legal advisor, don't you know,
> He said they can't stop us, so let her go.
> Here's to Woodrow Wilson, oh.

Wilson continued his yearly lecture course for graduate students at Johns Hopkins in which he expounded on his theory of government and how it was implemented in America and in Europe. Attending those lectures was Frederick Jackson Turner, the future frontier historian. Turner wrote his fiancée in the winter of 1890: "Dr. Wilson is here. Homely, solemn, young, glum, but with that fire in his face and eye that means that its possessor is not of the common crowd."

Through 1891 and 1892, Wilson devoted any spare time, including summer vacations, to working on the *Division and Reunion* manuscript. In early 1892, he was offered the presidency of the University of Illinois at Urbana. The salary was double what he was making at Princeton. Ellen and the children were visiting relatives in the South, and Wilson wrote her a frantic letter. "I need your advice desperately. It seems a . . . great opportunity. . . . I don't want a presidency, as you know, but I *must* increase my resources to provide for you and the children." He also sought advice from his friend Bridges, but it was Ellen's opinion that he valued the most. Ultimately, after many letters back and forth, Woodrow and Ellen decided to refuse the Illinois offer because they feared the position would leave him no time for writing.

The Princeton trustees, concerned that Wilson might accept other such offers in the future, voted to give him $3,500 to cover his housing and promised an increase in his salary as soon as possible. It was a wise decision on their part because, in the next few years, Wilson would be offered the presidency of seven different universities.

*Division and Reunion* was published in February 1893. Praised by critics, it established Wilson's reputation as a historian. In July, because of the book's success, he was invited to speak at the Chicago World Fair. He used the opportunity to present his unique ideas on education. Specifically, he stressed that students studying to be doctors, lawyers, or theologians should first complete a four-year liberal arts education to learn about history, philosophy, and literature before they narrowed their focus to their special fields.

Wilson was so impressed by the fair that when he returned home, he insisted Ellen go while he stayed with the children. (They had agreed when the children were born never to be away from them at the same time.) Ellen was reluctant, but she finally agreed to go, taking along her cousin Mary Hoyt.

The Wilsons' three daughters *(from left to right)*: Margaret, Jessie, and Eleanor. *(Princeton University Library)*

Margaret was now seven, Jessie six, and Eleanor (called Nellie) three. Wilson wrote Ellen every day describing his adventures with the children: "I find that I'm getting much more intimately acquainted with the children. Nellie comes to me now as she would come to you, with all sorts of odd little confidences . . . which delight me. It somehow touches me deeply to be both father and mother to the sweet little chicks." Ellen's brother Stockton was now teaching English literature at Princeton. "Stock," as Woodrow called him, was a cheerful presence during Ellen's absence. Despite a ten-year age difference between them, the two men had become close friends.

The Wilsons' home on Library Place in Princeton. *(Library of Congress)*

In 1894, Woodrow and Ellen decided to build a house of their own on the vacant lot next to the home they were renting on Library Place. Construction turned out to be more costly than they had expected. To bring in additional income, Wilson agreed to write a series of articles on George Washington for *Harper's Magazine.*

Classes, guest lectures, and multiple invitations to speak already left him little free time. Now, with the additional pressure of meeting *Harper's* deadlines, Wilson was pushed to the point of exhaustion. His father, as well as close friends, urged him to take a vacation. "Can we not persuade you to lessen your work?" one friend wrote. "It is clear, Professor, that you are unduly taxing your strength." However, Wilson continued his demanding harried pace. By May 1896, he had not only fulfilled his contract with *Harper's* but also arranged for the articles to be published as a biography titled *George Washington.* Though panned by the critics, the book sold well to the general public.

Then the constant pressure caught up with him. One morning in May, Wilson woke to find he could not use his right hand. Diagnoses varied from neuritis to "writer's cramp." He may, however, have suffered a small stroke, which would not have been recognized by physicians at that time. His doctor recommended an extended vacation.

Wilson had been contemplating a trip to England anyway, and Ellen, who would stay with the children, urged him to go. "I am counting so much on the sea voyage . . . the mental refreshment . . . the complete change from all the . . . exhausting demands upon you [to make you well]," she wrote him.

Wilson sailed for England on May 30. It was his first trip outside the United States. Aboard ship, he wrote letters to Ellen using his left hand. Before long he declared that his right hand, which he described as a "most promising patient," was improving rapidly. An avid cyclist, Wilson did most of his sightseeing from a bicycle. The experience, he wrote Ellen, was "exhilarating beyond expression."

He arrived home in September refreshed and rested. But despite claims to Ellen that his right hand was improved, pain still forced him to write with his left hand. He began using a typewriter, a recent invention, to save time.

In October 1896, Princeton held a three-day sesquicentennial celebration, marking the 150th anniversary of the college. Wilson was designated to make the keynote speech about the university and its future. His audience included statesmen from all over the world, important religious leaders, and Princeton graduates.

Wilson's words—as he no doubt realized—would have a resounding impact on his future at the university. Titled "Princeton in the Nation's Service," the speech summed up his ideas about a university's responsibilities to a democratic government. He stressed that students must be trained not only intellectually but must also be prepared to serve the nation through responsible political and social leadership. Emphasizing the importance of blending a liberal education with religious instruction, he said the university should teach young men to be "concerned with righteousness in this world, as well as with salvation in the next."

The speech, widely reprinted in national newspapers, attracted attention far beyond the Princeton campus. Ellen wrote triumphantly to Mary Hoyt, "It was the most brilliant,—*dazzling*—success. . . . And *such* an ovation as Woodrow received!"

Wilson took advantage of his growing popularity to request that Frederick Jackson Turner, then teaching at the University of Wisconsin, be hired for the history department. He believed the young professor's fresh ideas would invigorate the department. Initially, President Patton appeared to support hiring Turner, but ultimately he balked because Turner was a Unitarian and hiring him might jeopardize contributions from certain alumni. Wilson, who had urged Turner to consider the appointment in the first place, was so embarrassed and angered that he considered resigning.

In the end he remained at Princeton, but when the University of Virginia offered him a presidential position in the spring of 1898, he was tempted to accept it. He had a special fondness for Virginia, and two of his fraternity brothers—including his good friend Heath Dabney—were on the Virginia faculty. But friends and colleagues at Princeton urged him to stay. Finally, a group of wealthy alumni arranged to pay him, via personal donations, $2,500 a year over and above his salary. After such an astonishing show of loyalty and respect from his peers, Wilson could not leave.

His new financial security allowed him to devote more time to writing a history of America. He had started the book four years earlier but had often been forced to lay it aside in order to take on projects that offered more immediate financial rewards. Now, he worked on it steadily throughout the 1898 college term, stopping only to write occasional articles for major periodicals like the *Atlantic Monthly*. He earned more and more for such articles thanks to the popularity of his books, which had earned him a national reputation as a political analyst.

By summer of 1899, Ellen—always concerned about her husband's health—thought he appeared fatigued.

Ellen Wilson in Princeton in the 1890s. *(Library of Congress)*

She persuaded him to make a second trip abroad, taking Stockton with him. The two men sailed for Scotland in June. In their letters, Wilson and Ellen counted the days until they could be together again.

Wilson kept a diary for her, describing his travels. He and Stockton had taken their bicycles, and he wrote that he was "in love with touring and life in the open countryside." For her part, Ellen resumed painting, read the latest novels, and wrote that she had become "a devotee of pleasure." Knowing his love for baseball, she also kept Wilson informed about Princeton's team. "Now comes something *really* important . . . the result of the game," she wrote in one letter. "It was eleven to four in *Princeton's* favour!—sis! boom! ah!"

When Wilson returned, he apparently experienced a twinge of conscience that Ellen had been left at home so often while he traveled. He insisted that she take a trip herself, and in February 1900, she left on an extended vacation to visit friends in the South.

Two months later, Wilson signed a contract with *Harper's* for the rights to his *History of the United States*. It would be published in a series of twelve magazine articles, for which he would be paid the unheard of sum of one thousand dollars each. Throughout 1901, he labored over the articles. He had agreed to supply *Harper's* with "no less than ten thousand words per month."

His work was interrupted in the early winter of that year when his father became seriously ill. Woodrow went to Wilmington immediately, and when Dr. Wilson recovered he brought his father back to live with them in Princeton.

Meanwhile, college politics had continued to ferment. With school standards rapidly declining (athletics and membership in the campus eating clubs had become more important to students than learning), a small, well-organized group on the faculty started a movement to force Patton's resignation. Finally, at a faculty meeting on June 9, 1902, Patton succumbed to the pressure. Then, on a single ballot, without any other names being presented, Woodrow Wilson—who had stayed in the background during this power struggle—was elected unanimously to replace Patton as president.

A committee, which included Dr. Patton (who had recommended Wilson to be his successor), went to his home to tell him of his election. He was the first Princeton president ever elected unanimously.

Wilson received the news of his election with great joy. He knew that as university president he could extend his influence beyond the scholarly world. "In planning for Princeton," he would say in his inaugural speech, ". . . we are planning for the country." He believed that he had now reached the pinnacle of his career. "It has settled the future for me and given me a sense of *position*," he told Ellen, "and [it] . . . takes the . . . restlessness from my spirits."

# FROM PRINCETON TO POLITICS

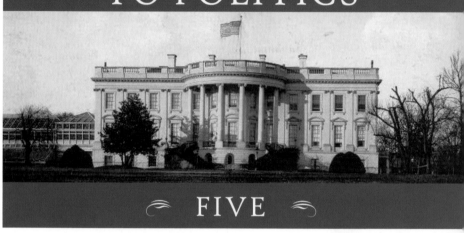

## ⌒ FIVE ⌒

Wilson spent the summer of 1902 working on the speech he would deliver at his inauguration as Princeton's president. "I feel like a new prime minister getting ready to address his constituents," he wrote Ellen, who was away visiting relatives. They were still living on Library Place, but come fall they would move into Prospect, the house provided for Princeton's presidents. Ellen called it "that great stately troublesome 'Prospect.'" She spent a good portion of the summer redecorating the huge mansion. By September, she had made it into a warm, comfortable home for her family, and a hospitable place for entertaining guests in the manner expected of the president of Princeton.

Younger daughters Jessie and Nellie shared a room, but Margaret, now sixteen, was allowed a room of her

Although Prospect, the imposing Italianate Victorian mansion on Princeton's campus, is no longer used as the residence of university presidents, the building is still in use as a faculty club. *(Library of Congress)*

own. The tower on the third floor, with three windows that provided a grand view of the New Jersey countryside, became Woodrow's retreat. He also enjoyed a book-lined study on the first floor.

On October 25, 1902—a golden sunshiny day—Woodrow Wilson, not quite forty-six, was inaugurated as the thirtieth president of Princeton University. The tiny village overflowed with visitors eager to witness the swearing-in ceremony. The Pennsylvania railroad had even arranged for a special train to run from Trenton to Princeton. The impressive academic procession included representatives from more than one hundred learning institutions. Financier J. Pierpont Morgan, writer Mark Twain, educator Booker T. Washington, and former United

States president Grover Cleveland were among those present. Theodore Roosevelt, the current president, had planned to attend, but he was prevented by a minor injury suffered in a carriage accident.

Wilson's inaugural speech, which emphasized Princeton's responsibility to produce "informed and thoughtful men," drew an ovation from the crowd. The Princeton football team made it a perfect day by defeating Columbia, after which a gala reception was held at Prospect.

Once installed as president, Wilson wasted no time. He had already met with the Princeton trustees. The situation, he had told them, was "critical." Academic standards had dropped, taking the reputation of Princeton down with them. Wilson recommended reorganizing the faculty, raising salaries, and building enough new dorms so that all students could live on campus. His major goals were to reform the undergraduate curriculum and institute a new teaching system.

Wilson's restructured curriculum would combine electives with required courses in order to ensure a more well-rounded education for students. The required classes would keep students from specializing in one subject to the exclusion of all others. Once the new curriculum was established, he wanted to set up a tutorial system like the one used in British colleges. Instead of students learning through lectures and memorized recitation, preceptors (young professors) would be hired to act as tutors to small groups.

Wilson's official portrait as president of Princeton University. *(Library of Congress)*

"The importance of the whole system," Wilson said, "lies in the character of the men obtained." He estimated that the tutorial system would cost $2.25 million. To help raise the money, he became what he termed the university's "official beggar," traveling around the country speaking to alumni groups and asking for contributions.

Addressing alumni in New York, he outlined his plans to transform Princeton into a "place . . . where there are [now] youngsters doing tasks to a place where there are men doing thinking." When he mentioned what the tutorial system would cost, some in the audience whistled. "I hope you will get your whistling over," he told them, "because you will have to get used to this."

Fortunately the alumni groups, as well as the faculty and trustees, shared Wilson's enthusiasm, and he finished his first year as president with a sense of triumph. He recruited fifty of the most promising scholars in the country to fill the new preceptorships. Most of them agreed to come because of Wilson's revolutionary programs and high ideals. Wilson faced little opposition to his proposals, and he enjoyed great popularity among his colleagues. On a personal note, however, the year brought sadness with his father's death at age eighty-one. Wilson wrote to a friend that he had lost his "life-long friend and companion." He accompanied his father's body to Columbia, South Carolina, to be buried next to his mother.

Much of Dr. Wilson's care had fallen to Ellen. She had hardly recovered from the strain of that burden when her brother Stockton suffered a nervous breakdown. She cared for him until his deepening depression required him to be hospitalized. Understandably, Ellen was exhausted. To raise her spirits, Woodrow planned a "second honeymoon." Their daughters, Margaret, Jessie, and Nellie, were now seventeen, sixteen, and thirteen— old enough to be left with relatives.

The Wilson family at Prospect. *From left to right:* Eleanor, Ellen, Jessie, Woodrow, and Margaret. *(Library of Congress)*

During their two months abroad, the Wilsons visited England and Scotland, then moved on to Paris, France, where Ellen reveled in the splendors of the Louvre. They returned home in time for the official opening of the academic year on September 23, 1903.

The next two years Wilson worked tirelessly at the university, but he did not forget his family. He knew that one of Ellen's dreams was to visit the great art museums of Italy. In the spring of 1904, when Ellen's cousin Mary Hoyt was traveling there, he urged Ellen to join her. She left in March, taking Jessie with her, while Margaret and Nellie remained with their father. He soon became both parent and nurse when first Margaret and then Nellie contracted measles. After Ellen and Jessie returned home in June, the entire family traveled to Canada to enjoy the rest of the summer together.

It was fortunate they had this respite because the new school year brought a series of misfortunes that tested the family's courage and faith. It began in December when Stockton was rehospitalized for depression. That same month, Wilson developed complications from a hernia operation. In the spring, Nellie became seriously ill. Then came the cruelest blow of all.

On April 26, 1905, Ellen received a telegram that her brother Eddie, his wife, and their young son had drowned in an accident. She plunged into the depths of depression, losing interest in everything around her. Wilson searched frantically for a way to help her. Finally, one of his colleagues mentioned an art colony in Lyme, Connecticut, where Ellen might find solace in her art. Wilson arranged for her to spend the summer there. In these surroundings Ellen's mental outlook improved, but it would be a long time before she recovered completely.

By the spring of 1906, Wilson—now forty-nine years old—was at the peak of his popularity at Princeton. The trustees and the faculty described him as "Princeton's most valuable asset." He never stopped striving to make the university the best in the nation. Between January 6 and May 19, he gave twenty-one speeches explaining his plans for Princeton and seeking funds to bring them to fruition. On May 28, the hectic pace caught up with him, and he woke to find he could not see out of his left eye. He consulted two prominent physicians, who determined that a blood vessel had ruptured in his eye. In reality, he had probably experienced a small stroke—possibly his second.

Wilson's blood pressure was high, and doctors prescribed total rest—the only treatment available. They also warned that he might never be able to return to work. The Princeton trustees insisted he take an extended vacation, and so Wilson rented a cottage in the pastoral Lake District of northern England. By the time he and the family sailed on June 30, some of the vision in the affected eye had returned, but he would never regain full sight.

The Lake District was an idyllic setting for recuperation. "No doubt God *could* have made a lovelier country than this Lake District, but I cannot believe he ever did," Wilson wrote his friend Bridges. He strolled along Grasmere Lake with Ellen or one of his daughters and took long walks through the lovely valleys and mountains. "I have tramped as much as fourteen miles in a day," he wrote his sister.

In mid-August, he consulted two specialists in Edinburgh, Scotland, about returning to work. Both told him it would be better for a man of his disposition to

Grasmere Lake in England's Lake District provided a perfect place for Wilson to rest and relax with his family. *(Library of Congress)*

resume work—provided he took reasonable precautions. They recommended he break up each academic year with a midwinter rest somewhere in a warm climate. "I have every [intention] to obey them," Wilson wrote a Princeton friend. "I love my work too much to be willing to run the risk of rendering myself unfit for it!"

In October, the family boarded a ship for home. Back at the university, Wilson resumed his reform agenda with fresh energy. On December 13, 1906, he presented a preliminary report to the Princeton trustees describing a plan to abolish the fraternity-like eating clubs on campus. He considered these clubs undemocratic.

In its early years, Princeton had forbidden fraterni-
ties on the grounds that they encouraged exclusiveness.
The ban still existed, but students had gotten around it
by forming eating clubs, supposedly to obtain better
meals. Over time, these clubs became more and more
aristocratic, filled with students from the school's wealthi-
est families.

Wilson wanted to replace the clubs with "academic
communities" called quadrangles, where students lived
and ate together, and where relationships would depend
more on intellectual involvement than on social ties.
"We have tutor and pupil. Now we must have pupil and
pupil in a comradeship of studies," he declared. The
board tentatively approved the plan.

While Woodrow handled university duties, Ellen took
care of matters at home. She had seen Jessie, now a
junior, and Nell, a freshman, off to college, and arranged
for Margaret—who had dropped out of college—to
study voice privately at home. Much to Ellen's delight,
the entire family was home for the Christmas holidays.
Unfortunately, joy turned to alarm when Nell had to
undergo life-threatening surgery for an infected gland
the day after Christmas.

By the middle of January 1907, Nell was out of
danger, and Wilson took the midyear break his doctors
had recommended. Alone, he left for a month's vacation
in Bermuda. Ellen stayed behind with Nell, who still
faced a long convalescence.

Wilson was captivated by Bermuda's beauty and

isolation. "Nations and all big affairs . . . seem here remote and theoretical," he wrote Ellen. In the same letter, he declared, "There is always the pain that you are not here."

While in Bermuda, Wilson met Mary Hulbert Peck, of Grand Rapids, Michigan. Unhappy in her marriage, Mrs. Peck spent her winters in Bermuda apart from her husband. She had a large house where she entertained all the prominent visitors to the island. On Wilson's last night there, she invited him to a dinner party. Mary Peck was a witty, vivacious, educated woman—in many ways more worldly than Wilson—and she fascinated him. He sent her a thank-you note the next day saying it was not often that he met someone he could "so entirely admire and enjoy."

Back from Bermuda, refreshed and rested, Wilson continued his drive to abolish the campus eating clubs. On June 10, the board authorized him to go ahead. But when a description of the quadrangle plan was printed in the *Princetonian Alumni Weekly,* it brought a deluge of angry protests. Wilson had made two mistakes. He failed to confer with the alumni, and he neglected to consult prominent faculty members like Andrew West. West, previously Wilson's staunch supporter, was now enraged by what he saw as Wilson's arrogance.

Despite the disapproval of West and a few others, the majority of the faculty supported Wilson. The powerful alumni, though, were another story. The battle continued through the summer as opposition to the quad plan increased every day. By September, it was clear that the majority of the alumni opposed abolishing the eating clubs. Not only did many of them have fond memories of their own membership in those clubs, they had also donated money to help build and maintain the clubs' elaborate quarters. With such strong resistance from their most prominent alumni, the trustees had no choice but to withdraw their initial approval; the university was dependent on alumni contributions.

Wilson felt betrayed, and it deeply troubled him that several longtime friends on the faculty had opposed him. As often happened, this emotional upset resulted in physical problems. In November 1907, he experienced temporary paralysis of his right arm. By January, his condition had improved, but he was more than ready for his second trip to Bermuda. Ellen stayed behind. Nell had recovered completely, but Ellen was concerned about her brother Stockton.

Back in Bermuda, Wilson renewed his acquaintance with Mary Peck. He was particularly vulnerable at this time, partly because of his recent professional defeats and partly because Ellen had been emotionally depressed and withdrawn since her brother Eddie's death. Wilson was an intense, emotional man, and Mary Peck was an attractive and unhappy woman. There is no doubt that Wilson had some kind of personal relationship with Mrs. Peck. Whether it was a romantic involvement kept on a platonic level, or whether it went further, cannot be determined with any surety. That Wilson later confessed

Wilson with Mary Peck in Bermuda in 1907. *(Princeton University Library)*

to "a folly . . . loathed and repented of" does not necessarily settle the question, because he would have "loathed" any betrayal of trust, on whatever level.

Ellen's letters from that period have been lost. But she apparently admonished him to be careful, because when Wilson wrote in one letter that he was seeing "a great deal" of Mrs. Peck, he added, "But I am remembering your injunction."

When Wilson returned to Princeton in February, he and Ellen somehow resolved the Mary Peck situation.

Wilson continued to correspond with Peck for several years about his political ups and downs, but he apparently avoided further personal contact with her. That summer, when he again went alone on a vacation, it was to England—not Bermuda. His letters from England suggest that though Ellen had forgiven him, he was still laboring to regain her trust.

> You have only to believe in and trust me, darling, and *all* will come right,—what you do not understand included. I know my heart now, if I ever did, *and it belongs to you.* God give you gracious strength to be patient with me! . . . I have never been worthy of you,—but I love you with all my poor, mixed, inexplicable nature.

If the storm clouds were clearing for Ellen and Woodrow, they were darkening over Princeton. The next two years would bring increasing turmoil and bitter disappointment.

In his installation speech six years earlier, Wilson had said, "We mean to build a notable graduate college . . . not apart, but . . . at the very heart . . . of the university." At the time, Andrew West agreed with that plan. Now, West—still angry about the eating club controversy—advocated moving Princeton's graduate school off campus.

The issue became a power struggle between the two men, and Wilson decided to tour the country and appeal to alumni groups personally. He was at his persuasive best, and it appeared he would win the battle.

However, on May 18, 1910, a wealthy Princeton alumnus died and left his entire estate to the university with the provision that Andrew West be in charge of how it would be spent. This left no question about where the graduate school would be located. Wilson chuckled when he heard the news. "We have beaten the living," he told Ellen, "but we cannot fight the dead. The game is up."

Wilson had restored Princeton's prestige among American universities, but the last four years had been a constant struggle. Now, with West in control, Wilson saw no chance of continuing his reforms. He would have to resign.

On the bright side, his speeches, books, and magazine articles on constitutional government had brought him national recognition. One man who recognized Wilson's political potential early on was George Harvey, the editor of *Harper's Weekly* and a longtime admirer of Wilson's work. As early as 1906, Harvey had put Wilson's picture on the cover of *Harper's* and touted him as future presidential material.

Now, four years later, Harvey—aware of the spirit of reform sweeping across America—thought Wilson's reputation as a reformer at Princeton could work to the advantage of the Democratic party in New Jersey. Consequently, he brought Wilson to the attention of "Big Jim" Smith, the political "boss" of New Jersey's Democratic party. No Democrat could succeed in New Jersey without Smith's support. He encouraged Big Jim to consider nominating Wilson as the Democratic candidate for governor in the upcoming election.

At first, Big Jim had his doubts about bringing in an outsider. But New Jersey had been in Republican hands for the past fifteen years, and Smith ultimately decided Wilson presented the respectable image the Democrats needed to regain power. Besides, he was certain the professor—naive in the ways of politics—would be easily manipulated. He asked Wilson if he would accept the party's gubernatorial nomination.

Wilson had long ago given up his dream of a life in politics. Now, suddenly, it was again within reach. In the language of his favorite sport, it was time to step up to the plate.

# THE JOURNEY BEGINS

## ⌒ SIX ⌒

In 1910, the year Big Jim Smith came knocking on Woodrow Wilson's door, America was wrestling with the problems created by fifty years of rapid industrial growth. The new economy drew people into cities, and as industry increased, so too did poverty. As some people thrived, others suffered. For the most part, African Americans were still considered second-class citizens. Women had few rights, and it was common for the children of the poor to work long hours in dangerous factories. Disease was rampant in overcrowded slums, while the rich enjoyed the sumptuous lifestyle of the Gilded Age.

A reform movement hoping to alleviate these inequalities began to develop. These reformers, called Progressives, planned to address the most urgent problems of the poor by instituting social and governmental reforms, primarily by eradicating political corruption and regulating business.

When Wilson considered running for governor of New Jersey, 2 percent of the population controlled 60 percent of the nation's wealth. Boss-controlled political machines dominated state politics. Big-city bosses kept these machines in power by purchasing votes and by giving jobs to important supporters. They especially targeted the huge number of immigrants flowing into the cities, promising them jobs or even buying them groceries in exchange for their votes.

When Smith and other New Jersey politicians met with Wilson about his possible candidacy for governor, their main concern was whether Wilson would go along with the Democratic machine or try to wrest control from the party bosses. Wilson assured them, "I have always been a believer in party organizations. If I were elected governor, I should be very glad to consult with the leaders of the Democratic Organization. I should refuse to listen to no man, but I should be especially glad to hear and duly consider the suggestions of my party." This statement satisfied the bosses, though Wilson's foes at Princeton could have warned them to pay closer attention to what he said. He never promised to do what they told him, only that he would listen to their suggestions. Asked to accept the nomination, Wilson said he would give it serious consideration.

By the end of June, Wilson was writing to Stockton Axson, "I am sure I can be elected Governor of New

Jersey. The convention meets in September, and I believe that I had better listen to the people who have been
wanting to present my name to it." On July 15, he
announced he would accept the nomination if it were
offered to him by a majority of the state Democrats and
with no conditions attached. But he would do nothing
himself to obtain it.

Wilson's nomination was hardly a sure thing. The
progressive wing of the Democratic Party thought he
was in the pocket of Boss Smith and the New Jersey
machine. Joseph Tumulty, a young Jersey City assem-
blyman who had long worked for corporate reform, later
described those suspicions: "We suspected that the 'Old
Gang' was up to its old trick of foisting upon the Democrats of the state a tool which they could use for their

Joseph Tumulty would become a loyal supporter and assistant to Wilson
throughout his political career. *(Library of Congress)*

own advantage, who, under the name of the Democratic party, would do the bidding of the corporate interests." Others did not support Wilson because he was a political unknown.

But when the state Democratic Convention kicked off on September 15, 1910, the power of the machine prevailed, and Wilson was nominated on the first ballot. It was by a small margin, however, and the angry progressive delegates—forced to accept a candidate they did not want—prepared to leave the convention hall. But when it was announced that the Democratic candidate for governor was present and would speak, most of them stayed to listen.

When he came on stage, they regarded him with stony faces. Wilson, understanding their hostility, quickly reassured them: "I shall enter upon the duties of the office of Governor, if elected, with absolutely no pledge of any kind to prevent me from serving the people of the State." He had not mentioned Big Jim Smith by name, but his audience understood he was saying that he would not be beholden to the party's political machine. Slowly the delegates—even the skeptical Tumulty—responded to Wilson's words and manner. The next day's Democratic newspapers crowed that Wilson was "the strongest candidate the party had offered in a generation." Even more encouraging for Wilson and his supporters was the positive response of Republican progressives—he would need their votes to win the election.

Telegrams and letters of congratulations poured in.

"The G.O.P. [the Republican Party] is in the soup!" Wilson's old friend Heath Dabney enthused from Virginia.

On October 20, Wilson formally resigned from the university. The trustees voted to continue his salary to the end of the year and invited him to continue living at Prospect. Wilson refused the pay, but the family did remain at Prospect until after the election.

He could now focus all his energy on campaigning for governor. In that campaign, he reiterated again and again that, if elected, he would see that the people were

During the campaign, Wilson appealed to voters with his honest, easy rhetorical style and fresh ideas. *(Smithsonian Institution, Washington, D.C.)*

FOR GOVERNOR

WOODROW WILSON

given a stronger voice in their government. And he stressed four specific reforms he would try to bring about: regulation of the rates charged by public utility companies, election reform to ensure all candidates would be selected by a primary election, prevention of election fraud, and enactment of a workers' compensation plan. Boss Smith—who opposed reform because it interfered with his interests—heard Wilson's promises but was not worried. He was certain that once Wilson was elected, he would be "practical."

Progressives in both parties heartily endorsed Wilson's proposed reforms, but they remained suspicious of the candidate's connection to Big Jim Smith's political machine. One of those skeptics was Republican George L. Record, a reformer and newspaper columnist respected by both Democrats and Republicans. Trying to determine Wilson's sincerity, Record sent him a list of questions. Wilson answered each one honestly and in detail. To the implied question of whether he would be controlled by the Democratic bosses if he were elected, he answered in a way that could not be misinterpreted: "If elected, I shall not, either in the matter of appointments to office or assent to legislation, or in shaping any part of the policy of my administration, submit to the dictation of any person or persons, special interest or organization." His answers were published in the New Jersey newspapers on October 26.

Two weeks later, Wilson was elected governor with the second-largest majority ever received by a New

Jersey gubernatorial candidate. Additionally, and just as important to the party, Democrats won control of the assembly, the lower house of the state legislature. Newspaper columnists nationwide noted the surprising victory of this Democratic governor in a state that usually voted Republican.

Wilson had not even been inaugurated before he faced his first challenge: who would be the next United States senator from New Jersey? At that time, senators were elected by state legislature, not directly by the people. However, in a preference primary, Democratic voters had indicated by a large margin that they preferred James E. Martine. The legislators, however, were not required to vote for the people's choice.

Boss Smith had previously served one ineffective term in the senate, but he had assured Wilson during the campaign that because of poor health he would never seek the office again. Now, however, with a Democratic majority in the state assembly, he was suddenly feeling better. He wanted to return to the Senate, and he expected Wilson's support. Wilson reminded Smith that the people wanted Martine and added that he would do everything he could to ensure that their wishes were upheld.

Smith angrily pointed out that Wilson could not have been elected without his support. Wilson acknowledged his help, but he again reminded Smith that the people had spoken, and that in his campaign he had promised to listen to them. When Smith insisted on submitting his name to the legislature as a candidate anyway, Wilson warned that he would do everything possible to uphold the people's mandate. Smith stormed off, furious that he had underestimated Wilson. Determined to win this fight, Big Jim sought out the other New Jersey bosses for support.

Meanwhile, Wilson talked to virtually every Democratic member of the assembly, urging them to support the people and not the machine. By December 8, he felt confident that Martine would be elected. Smith, however, still refused to withdraw his name. Wilson called on him personally to make one last try at persuading him to concede. When Smith refused, Wilson issued a public statement endorsing Martine. The fight with Smith was now out in the open. Wilson wrote Mary Peck, "I feel pretty confident . . . but a nasty enough fight is ahead, and I shall have . . . to go out . . . and conduct something like a systematic campaign against the whole gang: for Smith is only one of a gang that has had its grip upon the throat of the State for a generation." He had appointed Joe Tumulty, now an ardent supporter, as his personal secretary. Tumulty understood New Jersey politics, and Wilson put him in charge of the drive to defeat Smith.

In the meantime, on January 17, 1911, Wilson was officially sworn in as governor. After the ceremony he held an open reception. "All sorts . . . of people came," he wrote Mary Peck, "men, women, and children, and I felt very close to all of them, and very much touched by the thought that I was their representative and spokesman."

New Jersey did not provide a residence for its governors (other than a summer retreat near the ocean at Sea Girt). Wilson decided to continue living in Princeton and commute the twenty miles to his office in Trenton. His three daughters were now away pursuing their own interests. Margaret lived in New York and studied voice, Jessie worked at a settlement house in New Jersey, and Eleanor was in Philadelphia taking art classes. Three days before the inaugural, Woodrow and Ellen moved into four rooms at the Princeton Inn until they could find a suitable home.

Ellen Wilson in 1911. *(Library of Congress)*

The first order of business when the new legislature met was to elect a senator. On the first ballot, Martine— the people's choice—received forty votes, just one vote short of the number needed. Boss Smith, after receiving only ten votes, conceded defeat. Wilson refused to take credit for Martine's victory. "It is the people who are to be congratulated," he said. "All you have to do is to tell them what is going on and they will respond."

Less than a month later, the first of Wilson's four promised reform bills was presented in the assembly. Called the Geran bill, after a former student of Wilson's who introduced it, the bill provided that all candidates for office be nominated by public primaries rather than by party conventions. The New Jersey bosses, Democrat and Republican, fought the bill tooth and nail because it meant they would lose control of elections. Nevertheless, the bill passed in both houses. Passage of the Geran bill fulfilled Wilson's campaign pledge to return power to the people and made front-page news across the country. Some political pundits even speculated that he might be a presidential candidate in 1912.

In quick succession, the legislature passed a bill to limit campaign contributions and a bill that created a public utilities commission to regulate railroads and public utility companies. After only three months in office, Wilson had completed three-quarters of his proposed reforms. And he was acquiring a national reputation as a progressive and an anti-machine governor.

His fourth reform, one that had long been sought by

progressives of both parties, was a much-needed worker's compensation law to aid laborers injured on the job. It passed on April 3, 1911. Previously, a worker injured on the job had to prove negligence on the employer's part in order to receive compensation. This was very difficult, as courts usually ruled that anyone taking a job agreed to accept the risks that came with it. Companies, therefore, had no incentive to make working conditions safer.

When the legislature adjourned on April 21, George Record wrote in his newspaper column: "The present legislature ends its session with the most remarkable record of progressive legislation ever known in the political history of this or any other State." He added that without Wilson, "nothing of substantial importance would have been passed."

As national interest in Wilson increased, a group of his friends opened an office in New York—an initial step toward securing his nomination for president in 1912. In these early days, however, Wilson insisted the office was merely an information site. He told reporters there was "no campaign." And he cautioned his friends, "I am not to be put forward as a candidate for the Presidency. No man is big enough to seek that high office. I should not refuse it if it were offered . . . but only if the offer came from the people themselves." Despite such denials, however, he embarked on an extended national speaking tour in May. Appearing before clubs and organizations, he stressed the need for the common man to be freed from the tyranny of both big business and political bosses. Newspaper editors across the country soon referred to him as the new progressive Democratic leader.

Ellen's letters to Woodrow at that time overflow with pride. After reading several favorable editorials, she wrote him joyfully, "Isn't it all perfectly splendid and wonderful? It is like a royal progress. Surely you must be a man of destiny."

On June 6, Wilson returned home invigorated by the reception he had received across the country. He was now ready to admit publicly that he wanted to be president. By November 1911, campaign literature was going out to some 40,000 newspapers, libraries, and individuals.

It was a good time for a newcomer like Wilson to seek the Democratic nomination. The party was looking for a fresh leader. William Jennings Bryan had twice been the Democratic nominee for president and had lost both elections. He was still considered by many to be the party leader, but he had announced that he would not be a candidate again.

In late April 1912, the presidential primaries began. Candidates vying for the Democratic nomination against Wilson were front-runner James Beauchamp "Champ" Clark, who was Speaker of the House of Representatives, and Oscar Wilder Underwood, chairman of the powerful House of Representative Ways and Means Committee.

Wilson did poorly against these well-known candi-

Wilson's rival for the Democratic nomination, James Beauchamp "Champ" Clark.
*(Library of Congress)*

dates. However, he won enough primaries to keep any of his opponents from being nominated on the first ballot at the upcoming Democratic Convention.

Nevertheless, the situation looked bleak as the convention date neared. Champ Clark would go into the convention hall in Baltimore, Maryland, with 436 pledged delegates in contrast to Wilson's mere 248. (Two-thirds of the delegate votes, or 726, were required to win the nomination.) "Just between you and me," Wilson admitted in a letter to Mary Peck, "I have not the least idea of being nominated."

The Democratic National Convention met in Baltimore on June 25, 1912, to nominate the party's presidential candidate. Each state was represented by a specific number of delegates, depending on the size of the state. They arrived in a festive mood, hoisting banners and waving flags. Baltimore was experiencing a heat wave, but even the oven-like interior of the convention hall could not stifle the feelings of excitement and anticipation.

After the nominations were made, the party chairman took the first ballot, or vote, by calling the roll of states alphabetically. Balloting would continue until one of the candidates secured two-thirds of the convention votes. It was a tedious process that often required many ballots.

While the delegates sweltered in Baltimore's blistering heat, Wilson and his family enjoyed the cool breezes of Sea Girt. He would not go to Baltimore because he believed that no candidate should interfere with the convention process. His campaign staff, however, set up headquarters in Baltimore's Emerson Hotel. This staff was headed by William McCombs, a New York lawyer and former student of Wilson's, and William McAdoo, a Tennessee businessman who had become a trusted advisor. A direct, private telephone line installed between the hotel and Sea Girt kept Wilson informed of

The governor's house in Sea Girt on the Jersey Shore, where the Wilsons waited to hear the results of the Baltimore convention. *(Library of Congress)*

events on the convention floor. His secretary, Joe Tumulty, had accompanied the family to Sea Girt and would man the phones.

Missouri's Champ Clark, who ran so well against Wilson in the primary elections, was the convention favorite. He had the most pledged votes and was backed by the popular William Jennings Bryan. On the fourth day of the convention, Tammany Hall—the powerful political machine that controlled the New York delegation—cast all of that state's ninety votes for him. That gave Clark a clear majority, but he was still short of the two-thirds needed for nomination.

McCombs wired Wilson that Clark's nomination appeared inevitable. He asked permission to release Wilson's delegates so they could vote for someone else.

Wilson wired his consent, then cheerfully told Ellen, "Now we can see Rydal [the Lake District in England] again." Then McAdoo called and convinced Wilson not to release his delegates. McAdoo believed Wilson could still win the nomination because many progressive delegates, including Bryan, were unhappy about Clark's connection

Wilson's aide, William McAdoo, would not only serve in Wilson's cabinet but also become his son-in-law when he married Eleanor. *(Library of Congress)*

to Tammany Hall. McAdoo was proved right when, later that same day, Bryan switched Nebraska's votes from Clark to Wilson. The actual number of votes gained was small, but Bryan's action would influence other state delegations.

Day after day, the seemingly endless balloting continued, and the number of ballots taken neared thirty. The process was agonizingly slow because all forty-eight states had to be polled on each ballot. Finally on July 1, the sixth day of the convention, on the thirtieth ballot, Wilson passed Clark by five votes. A *New York*

*Times* reporter, one of several newsmen camped on the lawn at Sea Girt, ran to tell Wilson the news. "You've passed him! You've passed him!"

When Wilson showed no emotion, the reporter pleaded: "Won't you please let us see you excited just for one minute. We have written about the quiet pastoral scene down here till we simply can't do it any longer. . . . Now, please get a little excited." A smiling Wilson suggested that the reporter write, "Governor Wilson received the news that Champ Clark had dropped to second place in a riot of silence."

Meanwhile, in Baltimore, the weary delegates en-

Wilson receives congratulations in Sea Girt on his nomination as the Democratic presidential candidate during the summer of 1912. *(Library of Congress)*

dured twelve more roll calls during which the deadlock held steady. Then Roger Sullivan, the Chicago Democratic boss, delivered on a promise. He had told Wilson back in January, "I cannot say to you now what the Illinois delegation may do, but you may rely upon it, I will be there when you need me." On the forty-third ballot, Illinois's fifty-eight votes went to Wilson.

When Wilson's opponents charged that his staff was making deals with convention delegates in exchange for votes, Wilson issued a statement: "Of course I do not know in detail what my friends and supporters are doing. But I am morally certain that they . . . are not making arrangements . . . with anybody. There cannot by any possibility be any trading done in my name; not a single vote can or will be obtained by means of any promise."

Wilson may or may not have been that politically naïve, but certainly his staff knew that compromises, promises, and negotiations were necessary to win the nomination. They made a deal with the delegates still pledged to Senator Underwood. McCombs promised them that if it became apparent Wilson could not win, he would instruct the Wilson delegates to vote for Underwood. In return, the Underwood delegates promised not to switch their votes to Clark.

The strategy paid off. On July 2, on the forty-sixth ballot, Wilson was nominated. He received the news at 2:48 PM and went to tell Ellen, who was resting upstairs. "Well, dear," he said, "I guess we won't go to Mount Rydal this summer after all." Then they linked arms and walked downstairs to face the clamoring reporters.

Within an hour, a brass band arrived from the nearby village playing "Hail to the Chief." Horse-drawn buggies and automobiles lined the side of the beach road a mile deep. A crowd gathered outside the house, and Wilson emerged to acknowledge them.

His life would never be the same.

# TO THE WHITE HOUSE

## ⋐ SEVEN ⋑

In the weeks following the Democratic convention, the entire Wilson family struggled with the difficulty of living in the national spotlight. Reporters dogged their steps, wanting to know every detail of their lives. "The life I am leading now *can't* keep up," Wilson wrote Mary Peck. "It is inconceivable that it should. . . . Not a moment am I left free to do what I would [like]."

The family escaped the chaos temporarily when an old friend from Princeton offered them the use of his yacht. They spent a week cruising Long Island Sound, enjoying the privacy. Then Wilson had to return to his public duties. He had decided to continue as governor of New Jersey until he knew the outcome of the November presidential election.

In June, the Republicans had nominated the incum-

The Wilson family in Sea Girt in 1912. *From left to right:* Margaret, Ellen, Eleanor, Jessie, and Woodrow. *(Courtesy of the Granger Collection.)*

bent president William Howard Taft. But bitter infighting between Taft supporters and delegates who preferred former president Theodore Roosevelt caused a division. Republican progressives formed a third party called the Progressive Party and named Roosevelt their presidential candidate. This split in the Republican ranks was good news for Wilson and the Democrats. Ultimately, Wilson's main opponent would turn out to be the fiery Roosevelt, not the placid, good-natured Taft.

Roosevelt, who had been president prior to Taft from 1901 to 1909, was a formidable adversary. A colorful, charismatic man, he had been a popular president. In comparison, Wilson—the first candidate since the Civil War to be born and raised in the South—was relatively

Progressive Party candidate Theodore Roosevelt. *(Library of Congress)*

unknown. Even those Americans who knew what he had accomplished at the state level questioned how he would perform on a national level.

Although Wilson's positions on the major issues were usually more conservative than Roosevelt's, there were only slight differences. Both favored social and economic reforms that would break up the monopolistic trusts that controlled many of the nation's critical industries. While Roosevelt believed that a strong federal government should be empowered to regulate business, Wilson mistrusted federal power. He preferred legislation limiting the size of companies. Wilson's solution to monopolistic capitalism was less decisive than Roosevelt's.

In his early public appearances, Wilson was vague and unimpressive. Recognizing that he needed guidance, Wilson invited the prominent liberal lawyer Louis Brandeis to Sea Girt. Brandeis had made his reputation fighting monopolies and defending small businessmen. He helped Wilson clarify his ideas on ways to improve the nation's economy and destroy the monopolies.

One issue mostly ignored in the 1912 campaign was race. Segregation laws—the so-called Jim Crow laws—had been passed in the South and other areas, forcing former slaves and their descendents into economically powerless positions and denying them the basic rights and freedoms supposedly guaranteed to all citizens in the U.S. Constitution. Although the National Association for the Advancement of Colored People (NAACP) had been founded in 1909 to combat segregation, and though many prominent white and black Americans were opposed to segregation, neither Wilson nor Roosevelt made it an issue. It would be decades before the horrid conditions began to change.

Wilson launched his official campaign on Labor Day in a speech that called for the complete destruction of monopolies, labeling them enemies of free enterprise. He attacked Roosevelt's idea that the monopolies could be regulated by the government. "Once the government regulates the monopoly," Wilson said, "then monopoly will have to see to it that it regulates the government.

. . . Do you want to be taken care of by a combination of the government and the monopolies?" Noting that monopolies limited opportunities for small business owners, he promised to "take care of the little business-man and see that any unfair interference with the growth of his business [would] be a criminal offense."

Two weeks later, Wilson boarded an old wooden railway car and began a westward campaign journey, frequently speaking to crowds from the rear platform of the train. He would have preferred the quiet of a lecture hall,

Wilson campaigns from a train during his 1912 trip west. *(Library of Congress)*

but he made the best of the situation, often injecting humor into his speeches. Wilson loved limericks, and over the years he had composed any number of them for Ellen and his daughters. Now he used them so often in his speeches that reporters said he could come up with a limerick for any occasion. One of his favorites concerned his appearance:

> For beauty I am not a star;
> There are others handsomer, far;
> But my face, I don't mind it,
> For I am behind it;
> Tis the people in front that I jar.

Wilson began to draw large audiences. People liked the way he spoke. He never used notes, preferring to speak, as he put it, "right out of my mind as it is working at the time." Outside of an occasional joke, Wilson did not attack his opponents. Instead, he appealed to his listeners' moral and ethical instincts. He spoke of reform and the need for social justice. On September 18, in a speech at the Parade Grounds in Minnesota, he said:

> What I am interested in is having the government of the United States more concerned about human rights than property rights. Property is an instrument of humanity; humanity isn't an instrument of property . . . I say, therefore, that property as compared with humanity, as compared with the vital red blood in the American people, must take second place, not first place . . .

Wilson became known across the country for his animated and relaxed speaking style. *(Library of Congress)*

In every speech he emphasized the need for a free economic system. At his first stop in Indianapolis, he used the expression "a new freedom for America" in describing his plan. The press latched on to the phrase, and "New Freedom" became the slogan for his domestic program. As his train rolled through twelve states, the crowds grew larger and more enthusiastic with each stop.

Wilson returned home on October 12 exhausted but exhilarated, and pleased with the tour. Two days later, Theodore Roosevelt, en route to give a speech, was shot in an attempted assassination. A thick manuscript and an eyeglasses case in his vest pocket prevented the bullet from penetrating his right lung. Roosevelt, who relished this type of dramatic moment, went on to the auditorium and delivered his speech with the bullet lodged in his chest. "I shall have to ask you to be as quiet as possible," he began. "I have been shot. . . . The bullet is in me now so that I cannot make a very long speech." Then he spoke for an hour before he was taken to a hospital. If the Republican Party had not been so divided, that moment alone might have guaranteed Roosevelt's election.

Ellen immediately wired Roosevelt's wife Edith, expressing her sympathy, and Wilson wisely suspended all campaigning. By month's end, Roosevelt had recovered, and both candidates made their final pre-election speeches at Madison Square Garden in New York.

Election Day was November 5, 1912. Wilson and his wife and daughters waited out the night at their home in Princeton. A rented wireless telegraph kept them informed of election returns. Wilson led from the beginning. At 10:00 PM the bell in Princeton's Nassau Hall tolled, and Joe Tumulty called out to Ellen, "He's elected, Mrs. Wilson." Ellen ran to the studio room, where Woodrow stood in front of the fireplace, and kissed him. "My dear," she said, "I want to be the first to congratulate you." Though Wilson had won the popular vote by only a small margin, his electoral majority was the largest in history at the time.

A large crowd of cheering friends, neighbors, and Princeton students, many carrying flags and torches, gathered outside. Wilson came out on the front porch with Ellen and his daughters. He stood on a chair so they could see him. When the cheering finally stopped, the president-elect brushed back tears and made a short emotional statement: "I have no feeling of triumph tonight, but a feeling of solemn responsibility. I know the great task ahead of me. . . . I look almost with pleading to you . . . to stand behind me." Woodrow Wilson, once considered "slow" because he could not read, was headed for the White House.

# HOUR OF GOLD, HOUR OF LEAD

## ⧞ EIGHT ⧞

"I find myself after two years of continuous strain, rather completely [worn] out," Wilson wrote William Jennings Bryan after the election. On November 16, he retreated to Bermuda with Ellen and two of his daughters for a month of rest and solitude before taking office. They went sailing and picnicked on the beach. Some days Wilson bicycled around the island while Ellen painted landscapes of the lush tropical paradise.

He spent part of his time mulling over a list of potential cabinet choices. Some of the names had been suggested by the man who would soon become Wilson's closest advisor and confidant: Colonel Edward M. House. The men had met two years earlier when Wilson was governor of New Jersey, and they had immediately become friends. The Colonel said that after only a brief

Colonel Edward M. House. *(Library of Congress)*

conversation, they were "exchanging confidences which men usually do not exchange [even] after years of friendship." Wilson echoed this sentiment in a note to House the day after they met, writing, "My dear Friend, we have known one another always."

Wilson would come to depend on House's counsel, particularly in foreign affairs. The Colonel—an honorary title—had no desire to hold elected office. He preferred to work behind the scenes. "I can do my share of the work," he told Wilson, "and get a little of the reflected glory that I am sure will come to your administration."

In mid-December, the family returned home, and

Wilson went to work in earnest to select a cabinet. "I have been sweating blood over the cabinet choices," he wrote Josephus Daniels in a letter asking Daniels to serve as secretary of the navy.

He wanted to choose the best man for each post, but he was forced to restrain his natural idealism and face the reality of politics. One example of this difficulty concerned William Jennings Bryan. Wilson would have preferred not to have Bryan in his cabinet. But he could not ignore men like Bryan who had worked hard for the Democratic party. If he did, many Democrats in Congress would withdraw their support. He reluctantly appointed Bryan secretary of state.

Other cabinet choices were just as difficult. Many people he would have preferred for cabinet positions were serving in Congress, and he did not want to pull them out because he would need their votes to get bills passed. One sharp disappointment was his inability to name Louis Brandeis his attorney general. Too many Democrats, including Colonel House, thought Brandeis was too liberal, and Wilson was forced to back down.

He appointed one of his early campaign organizers, William McAdoo, secretary of the treasury. He did not, however, give a cabinet appointment to McCombs, his first campaign manager. McCombs, who coveted a post, had been loyal, but Wilson did not like him personally. He used McCombs's poor health as an excuse for not offering him a cabinet position and instead appointed him ambassador to France.

Thirty-three-year-old Joe Tumulty would continue as the president's personal secretary despite protests about his Catholicism. Wilson never showed religious bias toward anyone, and Tumulty remained with him through two administrations.

In the meantime, the family prepared to leave Princeton for Washington. On March 3, the day before the inauguration (the inauguration wasn't moved to January 20 until 1933), an automobile was sent to drive the family to the train station, but Woodrow and Ellen decided to walk. It was their way of saying good-bye to the old life. They took the long way, walking past the house they had built on Library Place and taking a last look at Princeton University, the scene of so many triumphs and defeats. At the station, they were greeted by a rowdy group of Princeton students who had asked to escort the president-elect to Washington.

On March 4, 1913, Woodrow Wilson took the presidential oath of office. He had promised during his campaign to serve the interests of the people, and on this inaugural day he felt the crushing weight of that responsibility. When a friend offered congratulations, Wilson told him prayer would help more.

Approaching the podium to speak, the fifty-six-year-old Wilson looked lean and fit. When he saw that the guards were keeping a large open space between the crowd and the inaugural platform, he directed them to "let the people come forward." The people surged to the front, and Wilson began his first speech as the twenty-eighth president of the United States. Ellen left her seat to join the crowd below so she could look up into his face as he spoke.

Wilson focused on the high price paid by society in a rapidly expanding industrial nation like the United States:

> We have built up . . . a great system of government. . . . Our life contains every great thing, and contains it in rich abundance. But the evil has come with the good. . . . We have been proud of our industrial achievements, but we have not . . . stopped to count the human cost, the cost of lives snuffed out, of energies overtaxed and broken, the fearful physical and spiritual cost to the men and women and children upon whom the . . . burden of it all has fallen pitilessly the years through. . . . There has been something crude and heartless and unfeeling in our haste to succeed and be great. Our thought has been 'Let every man look out for himself; let every generation look out for itself.' . . . There can be no equality of opportunity . . . if men and women and children be not shielded . . . from the consequences of great industrial and social processes which they cannot alter, control or . . . cope with.

The new president concluded one of the shortest inaugural addresses on record with the words: "This is not a day of triumph; it is a day of dedication. . . . Men's hearts wait upon us, men's lives hang in the balance; men's hopes call upon us to say what we will do . . . God helping me, I will not fail them."

Wilson delivered his inaugural address on March 4, 1913, to the press and a group of enthusiastic supporters. *(Library of Congress)*

An inaugural parade followed the ceremony, but the new first family cancelled the customary inaugural ball. It seemed an unnecessary extravagance to both Woodrow and Ellen. Instead, they spent their first evening in the White House with their daughters and the friends and relatives who had come to share their day.

The next morning dawned clear and sunny. Wilson began his first day in the White House with his usual breakfast of cereal and two unbeaten raw eggs swallowed whole in either lemon or orange juice. By 9:00 AM, he was in his office. One of his first decisions was to discontinue the "open door" policy he had maintained as governor. He could not waste valuable time talking to the hundreds of office-seekers hoping for government jobs. Even members of Congress were each allotted an exact period of time for talking to the president. If they were late, they lost their chance to see him that day. Joe Tumulty served as a buffer between the president and the many people who clamored to see him.

The days soon settled into a routine of cabinet meetings, personal meetings, dictating answers to correspondence, and meeting with the press. Wilson was the first president to hold regular press conferences. The president also wrote most of his own speeches, using shorthand for the first draft. He personally answered any letters that related to foreign policy, sometimes in his own hand, but usually on his personal typewriter. It was

Newly inaugurated Wilson *(front left)* with his cabinet during one of their first meetings. *(Library of Congress)*

a demanding schedule, and Wilson often worked late into the night.

Though he still relied heavily on E. M. House's advice, they both decided House should remain in New York. When Wilson sent for him, which he did frequently, House visited government departments and foreign embassies and then relayed his impressions and suggestions to the president. When the Colonel was in Washington, he stayed in one of the White House guest rooms and dined with the first family.

Wilson was not in office long before he learned the importance of party loyalty. He entered politics with high ideals, and to a great extent he never lost that idealism. As a result, he often thought in terms of black and white with no allowance for shades of gray, and this made life difficult for him. He found it hard to compromise in situations that he saw as moral issues but which his advisors saw as practical politics.

For example, he had a miserable time dealing with political patronage, the practice of rewarding past political supporters with government jobs. He was determined to appoint people—even for the most lowly jobs— on the basis of merit only. A case in point was the 56,000 postmaster positions to be filled around the country. He told Postmaster General Burleson, "I am going to satisfy myself that [those men] are honest and capable."

Burleson was horrified. Not only would the task have been an insurmountable one, but the Democratic senators and representatives in Congress—who used these appointments to reward supporters—would have turned on Wilson. "If you pursue this policy," Burleson told the president, "it means that your administration is going to be a failure." After further debate, Wilson reluctantly gave in.

As he had always done in anything he undertook, Wilson threw himself body and soul into his presidential duties. But he also understood the importance of holding on to his sense of self in the midst of these new pressures. He usually lunched in the family's private quarters with Ellen. In the afternoon he might play a round of golf or go for a ride in the White House limousine. Even though the car was chauffeur driven and a Secret Service man sat in the front seat beside the driver, these drives allowed him to relax without interruptions. Ellen sometimes accompanied him.

As First Lady, Ellen had her own duties, not the least of which was to make the White House a home. First families lived on the second floor in relatively small quarters. To ensure room for visiting friends and relatives, Ellen transformed attic space into extra guest rooms, reserving one room for a studio where she could paint.

On her first day in the White House, she looked down on the formal colonial-style garden below her dressing room window and told her daughters, "I'll change that. It will be our rose garden with a high hedge around it." Today, the Rose Garden is often used as a reception area by the sitting president.

The current White House Rose Garden, although redesigned under the Kennedy administration, still captures much of the feel of Ellen Wilson's garden, which was meant to evoke a seventeenth-century Italian garden, with rigid lines and formal green spaces.

Less than a month after his inauguration, Wilson made history when he appeared at the Capitol to address a joint session of Congress. It had been over a hundred years since a president had personally appeared before Congress. Previous presidents, beginning with Thomas Jefferson, had sent a written message that was read to the Congress by a clerk. "The town is agog about it," Wilson wrote a friend. "The President has not addressed Congress in person since John Adams's day—and yet what [is] more natural and dignified?"

However, Wilson also had political motives. He wanted the senators and representatives to see that he was "a human being trying to cooperate with other human beings in a common service." His first presidential goal was to pass a bill lowering tariff rates on foreign imports. He believed that high tariffs sheltered big business from competition and resulted in monopolies. Other presidents had tried to enact such a bill and failed. The problem was that congressmen faced extreme pressure from manufacturers in their home districts to vote against it. But Wilson's personal appeal to Congress proved a successful strategy. The tariff bill passed in September, and Wilson's presidency was off to a promising start.

That summer Woodrow and Ellen rented a house in Cornish, New Hampshire. They hoped to make it a vacation White House where they could relax and escape the stifling summer heat of the capital. Unfortunately, the tariff issue kept Wilson in Washington most of the summer. He insisted that Ellen go anyway, promising to come for weekends when he could. "I cannot choose as an individual what I shall do," he told Ellen. "I must choose always as President." But his long daily letters reveal that he was miserable without her.

Ellen thrived in Cornish. It was a haven for artists, and for the first time in a long while she worked seriously at her painting. When she began receiving artistic recognition, Wilson was pleased. In one of his letters he acknowledged the sacrifices she had made: "It is very wonderful how you have loved me. The soul of me is very selfish. . . . And you . . . who are so independent in spirit and in judgment . . . have been so loyal, so forgiving, so self-sacrificing in your willingness to live *my* life. Nothing but love could have accomplished so wonderful a thing." When he finally managed an eight-day stay in Cornish, it was like a second honeymoon for them both.

Ellen at Cornish in 1913.

In Washington, meanwhile, Wilson moved from one campaign-promised reform to another. On December 19, 1913—despite bitter opposition from private banking interests—Congress passed his Federal Reserve Bill, creating a banking system that would guarantee a more flexible money supply in times of economic crisis. He also created the Federal Trade Commission to oversee the day-to-day operations of big business in order to ensure fair competition and prevent monopolies.

On the negative side, Wilson's success was diminished by his relations with African Americans. Prominent blacks had supported him because he had promised them fair treatment. He did not follow through on that promise. Wilson could not overcome his southern white middle-class background. "A boy," he once said, "never gets over his boyhood, and never can change those subtle influences which have become a part of him." He continued to believe that blacks were intellectually inferior people who needed to be taken care of. Earlier, at Princeton, he had discouraged black Americans from applying for admission. (It would be 1948 before the first African American graduated from Princeton.)

Beyond Wilson's opinions on race, however, political motivation was also involved. Wilson was determined that nothing would get in the way of enacting his reform agenda. Because he feared repercussions and loss of support from southern congressmen, he appointed few African Americans to federal positions and allowed several government departments to be segregated. Though he claimed he believed segregation was beneficial for African Americans because it might spare them unpleasant encounters, Wilson's failure to stand up for equality or against discrimination remains one of the signal disappointments of his administrations.

A second failure of his first administration involved Mexico. The Mexican Revolution had begun a month before Wilson took office. General Victoriano Huerta seized power after assassinating the Mexican president, and the people revolted. European powers, anxious to protect their financial investments in Mexico, had no difficulty accepting Huerta, but Wilson refused to acknowledge him as Mexico's leader. "We have no sympathy with those who seek to seize the power of government to advance their own personal interests," he stated.

Instead he sided with the revolutionaries, led by the so-called Constitutionalist Venustiano Carranza. He hoped Carranza could establish a constitutional government in Mexico to replace Huerta's dictatorship. Wilson wanted to let Mexico work out its own problems, but his

Mexican general Victoriano Huerta. *(Library of Congress)*

extreme dislike of Huerta combined with his concern for the Mexican people ultimately led him to intervene.

In April 1914, when some American sailors were arrested and temporarily held at Tampico, Wilson used the incident as an excuse to send the navy to occupy Vera Cruz. Unfortunately, this resulted in the loss of both Mexican and American lives and the threat of all-out war. Wilson had not expected resistance, and he was devastated by the outcome. The three big powers of South America—Argentina, Brazil, and Chile—offered to mediate the situation, and Wilson jumped at the offer. War was avoided, and Huerta soon resigned, replaced by Carranza. However, Mexico would continue to be a concern.

Despite these missteps, Wilson's accomplishments during his first term were impressive. In two years, he pushed through more reform legislation than had ever been accomplished in so short a time. But then his private world was shattered.

The nightmare began in early spring when Ellen complained of excessive fatigue. Dr. Cary T. Grayson, the family's official physician and friend, attributed the tiredness to overwork. Not only had she been working hard as First Lady, she had also supervised two White House weddings. (Daughters Jessie and Eleanor had married within six months of each other.)

By July, however, it became apparent that Ellen was suffering from more than exhaustion. Sorrowfully, Dr. Grayson made the diagnosis of Bright's disease, a kidney ailment, "so far advanced that it was incurable." For several months Wilson refused to accept the diagnosis, insisting it was only the Washington heat that was bothering her. Finally, however, he could deny it no longer. In her last weeks, he never left her bedside. On August 6, with her daughters around her and Woodrow holding her hand, Ellen died. Wilson was devastated. Dr. Grayson heard him sob and exclaim, "Oh, my God, what am I to do?"

Ellen's funeral service was held in the East Room of the White House. Wilson maintained a stoic composure throughout, and then boarded a special train to accompany the body to Rome, Georgia, for burial. Standing at the graveside in a driving Georgia rain, the president broke down and "sobbed uncontrollably."

In the months ahead, only his faith sustained him. "I do not see the light yet," he wrote Colonel House three months after Ellen's death, "but it is not necessary for me to see it: I know it shines, and I know *where* it shines."

World circumstances allowed him little time to grieve. Just five days before Ellen's death, Germany invaded France. The First World War had begun. Ellen never knew. "We must be grateful," Wilson later told one of his daughters, "that she did not see the world crash into ruin. It would have broken her heart."

# MAKING THE WORLD SAFE FOR DEMOCRACY

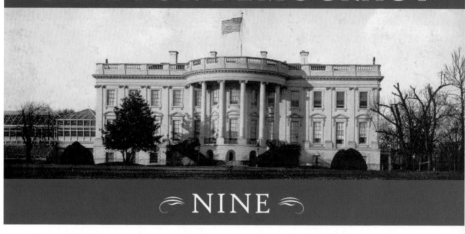

## ⟡ NINE ⟡

World War I, sometimes called the Great War, was the first to involve all of the major powers of the world. At the beginning, it pitted the Central Powers (Germany, Italy, and Austria-Hungary) against the Allies (France, Great Britain, and Russia). Most Americans felt this European war did not concern them and agreed with President Wilson that the country should stay out of it. On August 7, 1914, just one day after burying his wife, the grief-stricken president issued a statement that America would remain neutral. He offered to mediate between the warring countries, but all sides refused his offer.

Wilson urged Americans to be neutral "in thought as well as in action." This was easier said than done. More than one-third of Americans were either foreign-born or the children of foreign-born parents. The majority, including a large number of German-Americans, sympathized with the Allies.

Being neutral meant more than refusing to take sides. International law required a neutral country to continue selling noncontraband goods to both sides. This became a problem for the United States on February 4, 1915, when the Germans announced they were launching all-out submarine warfare against the British, using a new weapon: the U-boat (short for the German *Unterseeboot*). They warned that even neutral ships trading with Great Britain might be fired upon and destroyed without warning or regard for crews and passengers. Britain and France retaliated by setting up a blockade to prevent any supplies, including food, from being shipped to Germany.

A German U-boat is shown docked in Boulogne, France, during the war. *(Library of Congress)*

After being torpedoed, it took only a matter of minutes for the ill-fated luxury liner *Lusitania* to sink to the ocean's floor. *(Library of Congress)*

Wilson sent stern notes of protest to both sides, but Great Britain continued its blockade, and Germany began its submarine campaign as promised. A British liner sailing to Africa was sunk and 103 people were killed, one of them an American. Before the president could decide on a course of action, an even greater crisis occurred.

On May 7, 1915, a German U-boat torpedoed the British luxury liner *Lusitania.* In eighteen minutes the ship sank, taking 1,198 people down with it—128 of them Americans. On May 13, Wilson appealed to Germany to halt submarine warfare against any ships that were not vessels of war. Germany's response was less than straightforward, and Wilson dispatched a stronger and sharper warning. On July 31, he sent a third note demanding that Germany follow international law regarding unarmed passenger liners, which required that a passenger ship be warned before it was fired upon so those on board had a chance to disembark.

Secretary of State William Jennings Bryan, a dedicated pacifist, thought the president's warnings were too strong and would lead to America entering the war. He suggested Wilson simply prohibit Americans from sailing on ships in the war zone. But Wilson would not yield the right of Americans to travel unrestricted on the high seas. Bryan resigned in protest.

After the sinking of the *Lusitania,* German leaders tried to appease the United States—they did not want America to enter the war. Consequently, in August, when a second British liner was sunk and two American lives were lost, the German chancellor apologized. He promised that no more unarmed passenger ships would be sunk without warning. It appeared Wilson's patience had been effective.

On a personal level, the president continued to grieve for Ellen. In the bleak and miserable months following her death, he despaired of ever feeling happiness again. Immersed in a black depression, he forced himself to deal with the affairs of the country. "It is amazing," he said, "how one can continue to function in all ordinary, and some extraordinary, matters with a broken heart. I would not have believed it. But it is possible."

The prevailing gloom of the White House was lightened momentarily when daughter Jessie and her husband came to Washington, D.C., for the birth of their first child. Francis Sayer Jr., Wilson's first grandchild, was born on January 19, 1915.

Helen Bones, the president's cousin and sister of Jessie Bones, had taken over hostess duties at the White House. Three months after Ellen's death, Helen wrote a friend, "I cannot tell you how terrible this house seems without Cousin Ellen; and it simply grows worse every day . . . no one can offer Cousin Woodrow any . . . comfort, for there is no comfort."

But it was Helen who unknowingly helped Wilson find happiness again when she introduced him to a striking forty-two-year-old widow, Edith Bolling Galt. Helen and Edith often walked together. At the end of one such walk, Helen invited her to the White House for tea. It was a cold, raw day in March, and both women's shoes were covered with mud. Edith protested that she could not go to the White House in that condition. But when Helen assured her they would use the back entrance and that no one would see them, she consented.

As fate would have it, Wilson and Dr. Grayson were just returning from a game of golf. Edith stepped out of the White House elevator to find herself face-to-face with the president. He asked the two women to join him and Dr. Grayson for tea. By the time tea was finished, Wilson was smitten with the lovely Mrs. Galt. "It [was] the first time I had seen him smile since Cousin Ellie's death," Helen noted happily. And when asked how long it took for the president to be charmed

Wilson, a lifelong baseball fan, throws out the first pitch at a season opener. A smiling Edith Galt is seated to his immediate right. *(Library of Congress)*

by Mrs. Galt, she answered, "About ten minutes."

Throughout the rest of March and into April, Wilson frequently invited Mrs. Galt (always chaperoned by Helen Bones) to accompany him on his daily automobile rides. In mid-April, Edith was seated in the president's box when he threw out the first ball in a baseball game between the Washington Senators and the New York Yankees.

On May 4, less than two months after their first meeting, Edith Galt attended her first formal dinner at the White House. It was a beautiful spring night, and after dinner the president led Edith out to the south portico where they could be alone. To her shock and surprise, he told her he loved her and asked her to marry him. "Oh, you can't love me," she protested, "for you don't really know me, and it is less than a year since your wife died."

But Wilson was not one to give up. At his insistence,

she agreed to continue seeing him as long as a suitable chaperone was present. She had dinner in the White House at least three times a week, and occasionally they dined aboard the presidential yacht. He sent flowers every day, along with passionate love letters. "You are so vivid . . . . You are so beautiful!" he wrote. "You are my ideal companion . . . You are my perfect *playmate* . . . The old shadows are gone, the old loneliness banished." By August, they were secretly engaged.

Wilson's advisors and cabinet officers were well aware

Edith Bolling Galt. *(Courtesy of the Granger Collection.)*

of what was going on, and many, including Colonel House, were unhappy about the relationship. An election year was coming up, and they feared the country's reaction to the president becoming romantically involved so soon after his wife's death. House wrote in his diary, "It seems the President is wholly absorbed in this love affair and is neglecting practically everything else."

In an attempt to break up the romance, Wilson's son-in-law William McAdoo told him that Mary Peck had threatened to sell incriminating letters that would reveal their past relationship. This was a lie, but Wilson did not know it. He was devastated, mostly because of the pain he knew such a disclosure would cause Edith.

He went to her house to warn her of the impending scandal. A letter he wrote her the next morning implies that he also confessed his relationship with Mary Peck. He had come to Edith, he wrote, "stained and unworthy," guilty of "a folly long ago loathed and repented of." Edith was shocked, but she did not break off their engagement. "I will stand by you—not for duty, not for pity . . . but for love," she wrote back.

On October 8, 1915, the president's engagement was announced to the country. Now there was no more need for secrecy. Wilson dined often at Edith's house while the Secret Service waited outside. One of those guards, Ed Starling, wrote later that sometimes Wilson insisted on walking home rather than riding in the limousine. "I remember those October and November nights," Starling wrote. "We walked briskly, and the President danced

This card was issued in commemoration of the president's marriage to Edith Galt on December 18, 1915. *(Library of Congress)*

off the curbs and up them when we crossed streets."

Woodrow and Edith were married on December 18, 1915. Now with a loving companion once again by his side, Wilson faced the new year with renewed strength. He would need it. The bloodbath in Europe continued, and with Germany threatening submarine warfare, the danger of America becoming involved increased with each passing day. The president had twice sent Colonel House to Europe in search of a peaceful solution; now he tried again. House left shortly after the wedding, going first to London, then Paris, and finally Berlin.

Wilson also asked Congress for legislation to increase military preparedness in the event that America was forced to enter the war. In the spring of 1916, a bill was passed to strengthen America's armed forces. Meanwhile, the president pushed the German government to limit submarine warfare and to guarantee the safety of

merchant ships. But on March 24, 1916, without warning, a German U-boat torpedoed the *Sussex,* an unarmed
French ferryboat. Wilson threatened to break off diplomatic relations if the Germans did not cease their attacks
on passenger liners and commercial ships. On May 4,
Germany agreed not to attack such ships without first
giving them a chance to surrender. Despite Germany's
repeated broken promises, Wilson was willing to give
them yet another chance because neither he nor the
American people wanted war.

It was accepted that Wilson would be the Democratic
nominee for president in 1916. To run against him, the
Republicans nominated Charles Evans Hughes, an associate justice of the Supreme Court and a political
moderate. This time, Republicans were strongly united
behind their candidate.

With the outbreak of war in Europe, Wilson had put
much of his domestic reform program on hold. Now with
the election approaching, he resumed his progressive
agenda. He started by nominating Louis Brandeis to fill
a vacant seat on the Supreme Court. Four years earlier,
he had been forced to back down on a cabinet appointment for Brandeis. This time he would not. It was a
controversial appointment for two reasons: Brandeis
was the first Jew to be nominated for the court, and he
was known as a friend to labor. When the debate became
ugly, the president wrote a letter to the Senate Judiciary
Committee summing up his support of Brandeis: "He is
a friend of all just men and a lover of . . . right." Brandeis

1916 Republican presidential nominee Charles Evans Hughes. *(Library of Congress)*

was ultimately approved by the committee and by a full vote in the Senate.

In line with his personal vision of a world free of imperialism, Wilson pushed through a bill that promised future independence to the Philippines and allowed them more self-governing powers in the interim. The Philippines had been ceded to the United States by Spain after the Spanish-American War. He also pleased both labor and social reformers by forcing adoption of national child-labor laws and passing laws that guaranteed workmen's compensation for federal employees and an eight-hour workday for railroad workers.

The Democratic Convention was held in June 1916, and Wilson was nominated without any real opposition. By the time the convention ended, Democrats were using the slogan "He kept us out of war." Wilson heartily disliked it. "I can't keep the country out of war," he told one of his cabinet members. "They talk of me as though I were a god. Any little German lieutenant can put us into the war at any time by some calculated outrage."

On election night, November 7, 1916, Wilson went to bed believing he had lost. His opponent had already carried New York, and no one believed a candidate could win without New York. In the end, however, election results depended on the California vote. When the ballot count was completed, Wilson carried California by only 4,000 votes, but it was enough to reelect him. The vote was close enough that Hughes waited two weeks to concede.

Events moved quickly after the election. Wilson, hoping to act as an intermediary between the warring nations, asked the countries to state their conditions for peace. The Allies responded, but Germany and the other Central Powers did not. The German high command, unbeknownst to Wilson, had already decided to resume submarine warfare against all merchant ships, whether neutral or not. German leaders knew this would bring America into the war, but they hoped to defeat the Allies before America could rally to action.

On January 22, 1917, with war clouds looming, Wilson spoke before the Senate. What must be sought in Europe, he said, was "a peace without victory." A crushing victory for either side "would mean peace forced upon the loser . . . accepted in humiliation . . . and would leave . . . a resentment . . . upon which terms of peace would rest, not permanently, but . . . upon quicksand."

The British indicated they were ready to talk peace, but the Germans decided on a final all-out effort to win the war. German officials announced that after February 1, they would begin sinking *all* ships without warning. Two days later, Wilson said that America was breaking off diplomatic relations with Germany but would still remain neutral.

But maintaining neutrality was rapidly becoming impossible. First, the Germans sank the British liner *Laconia.* Shortly thereafter, the United States intercepted a telegram sent by the German foreign secretary to the Mexican government. In it, the Germans promised that if Mexico joined with Germany in war against the United States, Germany would see that Mexico regained its lost provinces—Texas, New Mexico, and Arizona— as its reward. Mexico denied having any interest in an alliance with Germany. However, in the American West and Southwest—where opposition to American involvement in the war had been strongest—the people, fearing for their safety, began to reconsider their antiwar stance.

Then, on March 18, three American ships were sunk and fifteen Americans killed. Wilson now had little choice but to declare war on Germany. On April 2, 1917, he called a special session of Congress to request a

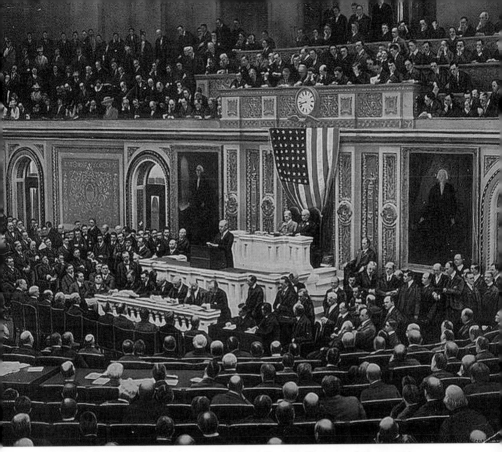

Wilson's speech to Congress emphasized the significance of the events unfolding and the gravity of America's decision. "With a profound sense of the solemn and even tragical character of the step I am taking and of the grave responsibilities which it involves," Wilson recommended that Congress declare war on Germany. *(Library of Congress)*

declaration of war. "The world," he said, "must be made safe for democracy." Americans would fight, he declared, "for the privilege of men everywhere to choose their way of life." He concluded his message with the words:

To such a task, we can dedicate our lives . . . everything that we are and everything that we have, with the pride of those who know that the day has come when America is privileged to spend her blood and her might for the principles that gave her birth. . . . God helping her, she can do no other.

Both houses of Congress overwhelmingly approved the war resolution.

Wilson was finally drawn into the war because he believed that maintaining a balance of power among nations was the only way to guarantee world peace. "As head of a nation participating in the war," he had told an antiwar group a month earlier, "the President of the

The last page of the United States' declaration of war upon Germany, bearing Wilson's signature. *(National Archives)*

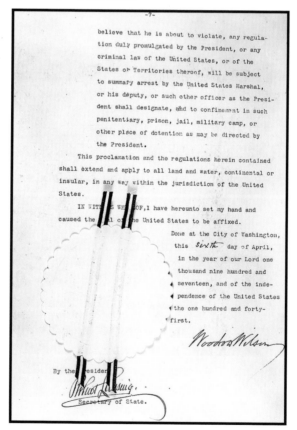

United States would have a seat at the Peace Table." As the leader of a neutral country, however, he would have little influence on peace negotiations.

On April 7, the president was at lunch when the declaration was brought to the White House for his signature. He left the table and sat at the chief usher's desk to sign. When he asked for a pen, Mrs. Wilson handed him a small gold pen he had given her as a gift. He asked her to stand behind him while he signed.

# WAR

## ⤚ TEN ⤙

Most Americans had no real understanding of what the declaration of war meant. The fighting was so far away and remote from their everyday lives. Many did not grasp that American soldiers would be sent to fight in Europe. It was assumed—even by some congressmen—that American involvement would be more in terms of financial support.

However, only three weeks after America entered the war, French and British diplomats arrived in Washington with an urgent message: the Allies desperately needed American soldiers. Consequently, in June 1917, Congress passed the Selective Service Act, which required all men between the ages of eighteen and forty-five to register at local draft boards.

Not all Americans approved of the draft. There had

been riots when a draft was introduced during the Civil War. The nation's army had been dependent on volunteers ever since. But an army had to be raised quickly, and a nationwide draft was the only solution. Even with the draft, it would be almost a year before American soldiers arrived in Europe in any substantial numbers.

The president had been so determined to keep America neutral that little had been done to prepare the people for war. Because of that, and because a significant number of Americans still opposed the war, Wilson

One of the thousands of U.S. recruitment posters generated to inspire people to volunteer for the armed forces. *(Library of Congress)*

appointed a Committee on Public Information to unite the country behind the war and to convey the message that the average citizen should expect to make sacrifices. Patriotic propaganda, including movies and pamphlets, was distributed nationwide. Posters encouraging enlistment in the armed forces appeared, and rallies where volunteer speakers urged support of the war effort cropped up all over the country. As a result, enlistment increased, and Americans were inspired to conserve the country's resources by honoring "meatless days, wheatless days and heatless days." Unfortunately, this newly aroused patriotic fervor soon spun out of control.

Although Wilson had publicly stated that America "had no quarrel with the German people," anti-German feelings surfaced across the country. Americans with German surnames were harassed. Teaching the German language was banned in some public schools. (Wilson called this "ridiculous and childish.") Even everyday language reflected this national hysteria. Sauerkraut, for example, became "liberty cabbage."

Wilson did not help matters when he urged Congress to pass the Espionage Act. This law, enacted on June 15, 1917, was meant to stamp out dissent and punish anyone who questioned the administration's policies. It even allowed the postmaster general to censor the mail for anything considered subversive to the war effort. While certain freedoms had been suspended in wartime before, it is difficult to understand Wilson's support of this assault on civil liberties—especially since he had always been critical of the loss of basic rights that occurred during the Civil War.

From the moment America entered the war, Wilson faced unrelenting pressure. The fact that he had a war to deal with did not cancel out domestic problems. Reformers, for example, still agitated for change. Women's groups were demanding the right to vote, sometimes chaining themselves to the White House fence to make their point. Edith referred to them as those "detestable suffragettes."

Wilson, too, disapproved of their tactics, but he was faced with the fact that the 1916 Democratic platform had endorsed women's suffrage. It was to his political advantage to uphold that platform, but he had also overcome some of his earlier prejudice. He admired the outstanding job women were doing in the war effort—many of them replacing men in the factories. "The women have earned [the vote]," Wilson declared when he requested Congress to pass the Nineteenth Amendment.

In other domestic issues, he opposed the Prohibitionists, who were demanding a ban on alcoholic beverages—although in this case his opposition failed and the Eighteenth Amendment outlawing the sale and consumption of alcohol was ratified. He continued to back labor by advocating an eight-hour day and wage increases to offset the escalating costs of living.

The war, however, took priority. In November 1917, an unexpected turn of events brought more upheaval in

Europe. The Russian government was overthrown and replaced by a Communist government headed by Vladimir Lenin. One of Lenin's first acts was to withdraw Russia from the war and make a separate peace with the Germans—leaving France and England on their own. The main force of American soldiers had not yet arrived, and the desperate Allies now needed them more than ever.

As troubles mounted, the only place Wilson could find peace was within his family circle. And those moments were becoming less frequent. "Just now there doesn't seem to be any private life left for me," he wrote to a friend at that time. Still, Edith was almost always at his side, even when he held briefings or signed important documents in the oval office. At Dr. Grayson's urging, Wilson played golf regularly, and Edith often joined him.

By 1918, the war had been raging for four years. On January 8, 1918, President Wilson called a special joint session of Congress to deliver a specific proposal for world peace. The message was aimed not just at the American people but at the whole world. The president recognized that the United States was becoming a global power and could no longer remain isolated from world affairs.

Wilson wanted to create a new world order based on democracy. His plan consisted of fourteen points. The first thirteen described ways to settle future conflicts without war. They ranged from doing away with secret agreements between countries to an overall reduction of

Edith, an involved and active First Lady from the start, stands next to her husband as he reviews a document at his desk. *(Library of Congress)*

arms. The fourteenth point described an organization that would provide an institutional framework within which problems between countries could be discussed and peaceful solutions worked out together. He called it a League of Nations. It was a dream he would fight for throughout the remaining years of his presidency.

# WILSON'S FOURTEEN POINTS

**Wilson's Fourteen Points, excerpted from the speech he gave to Congress on January 8, 1918.**

I.  Open covenants of peace, openly arrived at, after which there shall be no private international understanding of any kind but diplomacy shall proceed always frankly and in the public view.

II.  Absolute freedom of navigation upon the seas, outside territorial waters, alike in peace and in war, except as the seas may be closed in whole or in part by international action for the enforcement of international covenants.

III.  The removal, so far as possible, of all economic barriers and the establishment of an equality of trade conditions among all the nations consenting to the peace and associating themselves for its maintenance.

IV.  Adequate guarantees given and taken that national armaments will be reduced to the lowest point consistent with domestic safety.

V.  A free, open-minded, and absolutely impartial adjustment of all colonial claims, based upon a strict observance of the principle that in determining all such questions of sovereignty the interests of the populations concerned must have equal weight with the equitable claims of the government whose title is to be determined.

VI.  The evacuation of all Russian territory and such a settlement of all questions affecting Russia as will secure the best and freest cooperation of the other nations of the world in obtaining for her an unhampered and unembarrassed opportunity for the independent determination of her own political development and national policy and assure her a sincere welcome into the society of free nations under institutions of her own choosing; and, more than a welcome, assistance also of every kind that she may need and may herself desire. The treatment accorded Russia by her sister nations in the months to come will be the acid test of their good will, of their comprehension of her needs as distinguished from their own interests, and of their intelligent and unselfish sympathy.

VII. Belgium, the whole world will agree, must be evacuated and restored, without any attempt to limit the sovereignty which she enjoys in common with all other free nations. No other single act will serve as this will serve to restore confidence among the nations in the laws which they have themselves set and determined for the government of their relations with one another. Without this healing act the whole structure and validity of international law is forever impaired.

VIII. All French territory should be freed and the invaded portions restored, and the wrong done to France by Prussia in 1871 in the matter of Alsace-Lorraine, which has unsettled the peace of the world for nearly fifty years, should be righted, in order that peace may once more be made secure in the interest of all.

IX. A readjustment of the frontiers of Italy should be effected along clearly recognizable lines of nationality.

X. The peoples of Austria-Hungary, whose place among the nations we wish to see safeguarded and assured, should be accorded the freest opportunity of autonomous development.

XI. Rumania, Serbia, and Montenegro should be evacuated; occupied territories restored; Serbia accorded free and secure access to the sea; and the relations of the several Balkan states to one another determined by friendly counsel along historically established lines of allegiance and nationality; and international guarantees of the political and economic independence and territorial integrity of the several Balkan states should be entered into.

XII. The Turkish portions of the present Ottoman Empire should be assured a secure sovereignty, but the other nationalities which are now under Turkish rule should be assured an undoubted security of life and an absolutely unmolested opportunity of autonomous development, and the Dardanelles should be permanently opened as a free passage to the ships and commerce of all nations under international guarantees.

XIII. An independent Polish state should be erected which should include the territories inhabited by indisputably Polish populations, which should be assured a free and secure access to the sea, and whose political and economic independence and territorial integrity should be guaranteed by international covenant.

XIV. A general association of nations must be formed under specific covenants for the purpose of affording mutual guarantees of political independence and territorial integrity to great and small states alike.

Wilson's Fourteen Points were translated into a dozen languages and distributed around the world. Copies were dropped from airplanes into Germany. And people everywhere, even in Germany, sick of the killing and dying, responded with cheers. For a brief moment the world believed peace was within its grasp, that an armistice was near.

This hope was shattered when, on March 3, Germany announced the final terms of its peace treaty with Russia. This treaty left no doubt that the Germans were intent on dominating Europe. Wilson, bitterly disappointed, now told the American people there was but one choice:

"Force, Force to the utmost, Force without . . . limit, the righteous and triumphant Force which shall make Right the law of the world, and cast every selfish dominion down in the dust."

In May 1918, Germany made an all-out effort to win the war. By the end of the month, the German army had reached the Marne River—only fifty miles from Paris. American troops in France now numbered 500,000, with 250,000 more arriving every month. In July, when the Germans attempted to cross the Marne, the Allied and American armies forced them to retreat—a victory that turned the tide of the war.

In this allegorical painting depicting the end of the war, the figure of Lady Liberty leads the Allied troops to victory, with German refugees and prisoners of war in the foreground. *(Library of Congress)*

After four years of terrible war, the end came quickly. In October, the German government asked for peace. By November 11, 1918, the kaiser had abdicated and the new German government surrendered. The war was over. Only the peace terms remained to be settled.

"The Armistice was signed this morning," President Wilson said in his official statement to the country. "Everything for which America fought has been accomplished. It will now be our fortunate duty to assist by example."

Just six days earlier, midterm elections had been held in the United States. Going against his advisers, the president had made a personal appeal to the voters to reelect a Democratic Congress. A Republican victory, he said, "would certainly be interpreted on the other side of the water as a repudiation of my leadership."

Wilson had made a mistake. The speech not only outraged Republicans who had supported the war, but it offended many Americans who did not like partisan politics being injected into foreign policy. As a result, Republicans regained control of both houses. The Republican majority in the Senate was by only one, but in the days to come, that would be enough.

The war was over, but for Wilson the real battle was just beginning. Peace terms still remained to be settled. He had remained firm in his belief that although Germany must be defeated, it must not be destroyed or humiliated by the victors. He believed passionately that only a League of Nations—one that included Germany—

could ensure a permanent world peace. Because of these strong convictions, and because he knew the Allies would be seeking revenge against the Germans, Wilson felt a moral obligation to be present at the peace negotiations to be held in Paris.

Trusted associates and friends, including longtime supporter journalist Frank Cobb, advised him not to attend the peace conference. In a memo to Colonel House, Cobb warned prophetically, "The moment the President sits at the [council] table with these Prime Ministers and Foreign Secretaries, he has lost all the power that comes from distance and detachment. Instead of remaining the great arbiter of human freedom he becomes merely a negotiator dealing with other negotiators."

But the president was determined. "I believe in a Divine Providence," he told Secretary Tumulty. "It is my belief that no body of men [whatever] their power or their influence can defeat this great world enterprise." He would be at the peace table in Paris.

# PEACEMAKER

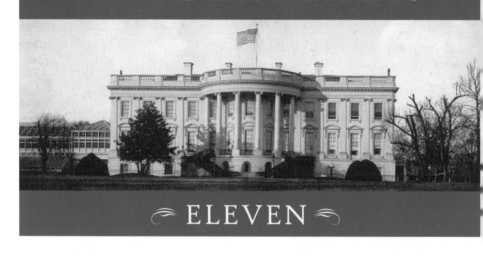

## ⟨ ELEVEN ⟩

On December 4, 1918, President Wilson and the First Lady sailed for France aboard the *George Washington*. No other American president had ever traveled outside the United States while in office. Wilson's critics complained that he was not satisfied with being president of the United States, he wanted to be "president of the World."

The president was accompanied by a group of advisors consisting of university professors and experts from various fields. He had also appointed four peace delegates who would sit with him at the Paris conference table during negotiations. One of the four was a Republican, but no Republican senator was chosen. This was a political mistake because the Republican-dominated Senate would have to approve any treaty Wilson negotiated. Senate Majority Leader Henry Cabot Lodge, in particular, would not forget this slight.

The president's political foes also criticized him for taking Edith along, but he needed her beside him. The ten-day sea voyage, described by Edith as "life-giving to my husband," was a rejuvenating experience for them both. Exhausted and ill with a cold when he first boarded, Wilson's health improved with each day at sea.

The *George Washington* sailed into the French port of Brest on December 13, 1918. From streets and rooftops, people welcomed the president, cheering and waving flags. In Paris, his reception was even more astonishing. The entire city was draped with flags and laurel wreaths, and 100,000 people jammed the streets, press-

Enthusiastic crowds greet Wilson upon his arrival in Paris in December 1918. *(Courtesy of the Granger Collection.)*

ing against the police lines, trying to touch him. Weary of war, they believed Wilson possessed the key to lasting peace.

The scars of war were visible throughout the city. Heaps of rubble and buildings with boarded-up windows lined the streets of bombed areas. Soldiers who had been blinded in battle or had lost arms or legs begged on street corners. Food was scarce, and coal, needed for heat, was in short supply.

Preparations for the peace conference were not yet complete, and French officials wanted Wilson to tour war-devastated areas during the interval. But he refused. He did not want to see what the Germans had destroyed for fear that he would lose his determination to make a just and unbitter peace. Instead, he used the time to review the American troops stationed near Paris. With Edith by his side, he visited the hospital in Neuilly, pausing at the bedsides of hundreds of wounded American soldiers. They traveled to England and Italy, where they received the same enthusiastic receptions as in France. By the second week of January, they were back in Paris.

The peace conference convened on January 18, 1919, and representatives from twenty-nine allied and associated powers attended the opening session. However, they would not all be involved in the day-to-day drafting of the treaty. With representatives from so many nations, each with their own advisors, it would have been impossible to get anything accomplished. Consequently, it

The "Big Four" in the Hotel Crillon, Paris, December 1918. *Seated from left to right:* Orlando of Italy, Lloyd George of Great Britain, Clemenceau of France, and Woodrow Wilson. *(Courtesy of the Granger Collection.)*

was decided to form a Council of Ten, consisting of two delegates each from the United States, France, Great Britain, Italy, and Japan. This Council of Ten would control negotiations. (Representatives of other countries would be invited to join negotiations only when their country's interests were involved.)

Ultimately, however, a Council of Four—Lloyd George, the prime minister of Great Britain; Premier Georges Clemenceau of France; Premier Vittorio Orlando of Italy; and Wilson—would make most of the major decisions. Once the treaty was completed, the entire assembly would vote on it.

European delegates wanted to settle the peace terms first and then call a second conference to work on a League of Nations covenant or charter. Wilson insisted that the league charter be a part of the peace treaty because he feared that once the Germans were disarmed the Allies would push the league aside. "We have assembled for two purposes," he told the delegates, "to make the settlements which have been rendered necessary by this war, and also to secure the peace of the world. . . . The League of Nations seems to me to be necessary for both these purposes."

Wilson stood firm against sometimes bitter opposition, and on January 25 he was rewarded. That day the conference delegates agreed to include the league as part of the peace settlement. A committee, chaired by Wilson, was appointed to work out the terms of the covenant. Wilson promised that a draft would be ready in two weeks, and he worked long, exhausting hours to make that happen. He drove himself relentlessly because he believed that the league would be the salvation of the world. His philosophy was that if people could be made to sit together and talk in a reasonable way, problems could be solved without wars.

On February 14, 1919, with all delegates present, Wilson jubilantly presented a draft of the completed charter to the peace conference. The league would consist of a general assembly with representatives from all nations, but only the larger countries would have permanent seats. There would be a clerical staff in Geneva,

Switzerland. The heart of the covenant was Article X, which committed league members to protect each other against outside aggression.

The league charter, Wilson told the delegates, was "a living thing . . . a definite guarantee of peace . . . against the things which have just come near [to] bringing the whole structure of civilization into ruin." He then read the document aloud. Colonel House noted in his diary, "It was indeed a moment of triumph for the American President."

The next day, Wilson sailed for America because there were affairs he needed to attend to at home. He would return to the peace conference, but for now he was

This political cartoon from 1919 illustrates Wilson's commitment to the League of Nations. *(Courtesy of the Granger Collection.)*

content to leave Colonel House in charge of the American delegation.

Once back in Washington, Wilson worked to gain the Senate's support for the League of Nations. He decided not to address the entire Congress. Instead, he invited members of the Senate and House Foreign Affairs Committees (including its chairman, Senator Lodge) to a private dinner meeting. Over dinner, Wilson explained the details of the league covenant. He answered questions until almost midnight, trying to quell the fear that membership in the League of Nations would force Americans to fight the wars of foreigners. But it was a futile effort.

Two days later, Senator Lodge—Wilson's most fervent antagonist—launched a full-scale attack against the League of Nations in an angry speech to the Senate. He demanded that the president justify how the league could possibly be compatible with the Monroe Doctrine. In that statement of foreign policy, made in 1823, America had vowed to stay out of the internal affairs of European nations.

Lodge did not stop with a speech. On March 4, he made public a round-robin letter signed by thirty-nine Republican members of the Senate. It basically stated they would not approve any treaty that included the League of Nations unless changes were made to the league charter. Congress was due to adjourn that same day, and Lodge kept a Republican filibuster going until it was time for adjournment. The result was that urgent legislation—the very bills the president had returned home to sign—was left pending.

Humiliated, Wilson angrily attacked the Republican leadership. "A group of men in the Senate," he stormed, "have deliberately chosen to embarrass the administration of the Government . . . and to make arbitrary use of the powers intended to be employed in the interests of the people." He then left with Edith to return to the peace conference in Paris.

Wilson's rival, Henry Cabot Lodge. *(Library of Congress)*

On the return voyage to France, Wilson fell ill with a fever. He joked that his illness was caused from "a retention of gases generated by the Republican Senators—and that's enough to poison any man." After several days, however, he recovered enough to appear on deck for a game of shuffleboard with Edith.

Colonel House was waiting when the ship docked in France. He met with the president and briefed him on what had happened during his absence. Edith would write later that her husband emerged from that meeting "looking ten years older. His jaw," she said, "was set in that way it had when he was making [a] superhuman effort to control himself."

He told her bitterly, "House has given away everything I had won before we left Paris. He has compromised on every side, and so I shall have to start all over again." Unforgivably, House had allowed the League of Nations to be pushed into the background of negotiations while Wilson was away. House's explanation was that the European leaders were aware of the Senate's opposition to the league, and he had feared they might withdraw their approval completely if concessions were not made. House's actions marked the beginning of the end for the long-standing friendship between the two men.

For two weeks, Wilson worked fifteen-hour days until he won back what House had bargained away. But the physical and mental stress took its toll, and on April 3, he became violently ill. For several weeks, he ran a 103-degree temperature and suffered with a raspy cough and a raging headache. The exact nature of his illness is still uncertain. Influenza, encephalitis, and a possible stroke have all been suggested.

Wilson ultimately recovered enough to rejoin the ongoing peace negotiations. At last, on June 28, 1919, the peace treaty was signed at the palace of Versailles.

*Opposite:* This painting by Sir William Orpen depicts the signing of the peace treaty in the famed Hall of Mirrors in the palace at Versailles. Wilson is third from the left of those seated at the table. *(The Imperial War Museum, London)*

Wilson had been forced to compromise on numerous issues. For example, under pressure from French premier Clemenceau and British prime minister Lloyd George, he had no choice but to concede that Germany must admit its war guilt and pay for the damage it had inflicted. This punishment would bankrupt the German economy, but without this compromise the conference would have self-destructed. It was not the peace-without-victory solution Wilson had sought, however, and the Germans—who had surrendered on the basis of his Fourteen Points—felt betrayed.

Nonetheless, the treaty was less vindictive than one the Allies might have adopted without Wilson's influence. He had sought self-determination—the right to choose one's own government—for the oppressed minorities of Europe, and he managed to secure it for several national groups within the German and Austrian empires by creating the countries of Czechoslovakia, Poland, and Yugoslavia. But the triumph that outweighed all others in Wilson's mind was that the League of Nations remained a part of the treaty. He was confident the treaty's weaknesses could eventually be corrected by the league.

On June 29, the day after the treaty was signed, the president sailed for home. Colonel House was there to bid him farewell. They would never meet or speak again.

At home, Wilson needed to persuade the Senate to approve the treaty despite some senators' reservations about America's involvement in the League of Nations.

On July 10, Wilson, his face drawn and lined with fatigue, submitted the peace treaty (now known as the Treaty of Versailles) to the Senate for approval. "Dare we reject it," he asked the senators, "and break the heart of the world?" He knew he could count on most of the Senate Democrats to vote for ratification, but he needed Republican votes to reach the required two-thirds majority. Standing in the way was his bitter foe, Henry Cabot Lodge.

Senator Lodge wanted Article X of the treaty, which required all league members to defend and protect each other, amended to say that the United States would not defend other league nations unless Congress approved. Wilson argued that such an amendment would open the floodgates for every nation to add stipulations, which would destroy the whole idea and spirit of the league.

On July 19, Wilson boarded the presidential yacht for a much-needed weekend of rest. He remained in bed the entire two days. Dr. Grayson told the press that Wilson was suffering from dysentery, but he may have had another small stroke. Although his recuperative powers remained exceptional and he bounced back quickly, these transient strokes affected him physically and mentally. Lapses in memory were becoming noticeable to those around him, and his headaches had increased in frequency and intensity.

Nevertheless, he worked tirelessly to ensure ratification of the treaty. In the remaining weeks of July, he met privately with eleven Republican senators he thought could be convinced to vote for the treaty. Then, on August 19, he met with Lodge and the Senate Foreign Relations Committee in a three-and-one-half-hour session. During this difficult encounter, Wilson kept his temper under control and patiently answered whatever questions the senators posed.

When these efforts failed to win the support he needed, and as Lodge—supported by other isolationist senators—continued to use delaying tactics in the Senate, Wilson made a fateful decision. He decided to take his case to the people. He would tour the United States to plead the cause of the League of Nations. A majority of Americans already approved of the league, but if Wilson could rouse public opinion even more, the Senate would be forced to ratify the treaty with the league charter intact.

Neither Edith nor Dr. Grayson wanted him to make the trip because of his precarious health. But when Grayson pleaded with him not to go, Wilson told him, "I promised our soldiers that it was a war to end wars; and if I do not do all in my power to put the treaty in effect, I will . . . never [be] able to look those boys in the eye." Grayson later wrote, "There was nothing I could do except to go with him and take such care of him as I could."

On September 3, 1919, a special presidential train left Washington. Seven coaches long, it carried presidential aides, Secret Service men, and reporters. The last car was reserved for the president and the First Lady. Dr. Grayson and Joe Tumulty, Wilson's private secretary, were nearby.

On one of the many stops during his ambitious trip to promote the League of Nations, Wilson speaks to a crowd of 50,000 at San Diego Stadium in California. *(Library of Congress)*

The tour was to cover 10,000 miles in twenty-seven days. As always, Wilson enjoyed interacting with the people. However, as the trip progressed, the sixty-three-year-old president's strength began to fail, and he endured excruciating headaches. Edith wrote in her diary that he was "suffering very serious fatigue." She begged him to return to Washington, but he would not. He knew that with every stop he was winning more support. "The people . . . are eager to hear what the League stands for. I should fail in my duty if I disappointed them," he told her.

In a speech on September 11, he stressed America's responsibility to the rest of the world. "America is going to grow more and more powerful," he said, "and the more powerful she is the more inevitable it is that she should be trustee for the peace of the world."

On September 25 in Pueblo, Colorado, he gave one of his most stirring speeches. "There is one thing," he said, "that the American people always . . . extend their hand to, and that is the truth of justice and of liberty and of peace. . . . That truth . . . is going to lead us, and through us the world out into pastures of quietness and peace such as the world never dreamed of before." He was in tears by the end, as were many in the crowd. It was the last public speech he would ever make.

The train's next scheduled stop was Wichita, Kansas. But during the night Wilson called to Edith, who was sleeping in an adjoining compartment, that he felt "terribly sick." He complained of unbearable pain in his head. Edith summoned Dr. Grayson, but he could do little to relieve the pain. The First Lady sat with her husband until dawn, when he finally fell asleep. "It was the longest and most heartbreaking [night] of my life," she later recalled.

Wilson awoke after two hours sleep, determined to prepare for his Wichita speech. But Dr. Grayson, along with Edith and Tumulty, finally convinced the obviously ill president that he must give up the tour. He had traveled 8,000 miles in twenty-two days and delivered thirty-two major speeches. Over and over again he had hammered home the point that without American participation and leadership, the League of Nations would fail. And without the League, there could be no hope for lasting world peace. In Pueblo, he had told the crowd:

> Nothing brings a lump into my throat quicker on this journey . . . than to see the . . . children . . . because I know that, if . . . we should not win this great fight for the League of Nations, it would be their death warrant. They belong to the generation which would then have to fight the final war, and in that final war there would not be merely seven and a half million men slain. The very existence of civilization would be in the balance.

With every speech, Wilson had gained support for the league. If he could have continued on the tour, the story might have had a different ending.

On October 2, four days after the presidential train arrived back in Washington, Edith found the president unconscious on the floor of his bathroom. He had suffered a massive stroke that paralyzed his left side.

# JOURNEY'S END

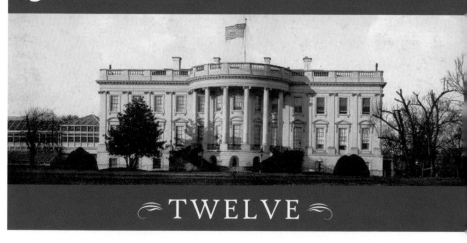

## ～ TWELVE ～

Dr. Grayson's statements to the press implied that the president was suffering from overwork and exhaustion. There was no mention of paralysis or stroke. Grayson later stated that Edith Wilson had insisted on secrecy. Only the vice president and the cabinet members knew how incapacitated Wilson really was.

For a full month after the October 2nd stroke, the president was unable to carry out his official duties. His speech was slurred and his left arm and leg paralyzed. In addition, he nearly died from a kidney malfunction. Since no one but the president's family and Dr. Grayson were allowed to see him, it is impossible to determine how much he was affected mentally. Some historians have suggested that during this period Edith ran the country—a charge she later denied.

Wilson's trusted physician and friend, Dr. Cary Grayson. *(Library of Congress)*

Whatever the exact truth of Edith's involvement, she did not deny that she controlled access to the president. "Woodrow Wilson was my beloved husband whose life I was trying to save . . . after that he was the President of the United States," she wrote.

By the end of October, Wilson's condition had improved, but he remained secluded. Finally, in December, the Senate Republicans demanded to see the president to verify that he was competent to remain in office. A meeting was scheduled for December 9, 1919. Two senators came to the president's quarters: Senator Albert Fall, a New Mexico Republican who was hostile to Wilson, and Nebraska Democrat Senator Gilbert Hitchcock, who was a friend.

On the appointed day, the two senators were escorted into Wilson's dimly lit bedroom. He lay on his bed, propped up by pillows, his paralyzed left arm covered with a blanket. The president, summoning his iron will, rose to the occasion. The visit lasted for forty minutes. As the two men were leaving, Senator Fall turned and said, "We've been praying for you, sir." Wilson retorted, "Which way, Senator?"

Wilson would serve out the remainder of his term, but he was only a pale shadow of his former self. Only here and there did flashes of the old vitality and brilliance surface.

Between November 1919 and March 1920, the Versailles peace treaty was put to a vote before the Senate three times. The first two times it was presented with Senator Lodge's fourteen amendments or reservations attached—one for each of Wilson's Fourteen Points. Lodge's reservations would have limited American ob-

Edith and Woodrow take a ride in an automobile in one of Wilson's first appearances after his illness. *(Library of Congress)*

ligations under the treaty. The Senate Democrats, instructed by Wilson to vote against it, defeated it both times.

For both Wilson and Lodge, the main sticking point was Article X. Some of Wilson's close advisers and even Edith urged him to compromise and accept Lodge's reservations in order to get some form of the treaty passed. His answer was: "Let Lodge compromise." But neither of the two men would budge. On March 19, 1920, the Senate—pressured by public opinion—voted on the treaty without Lodge's reservations attached. This time it was defeated by the Republicans. It would not be voted on again. When Tumulty told Wilson about the Senate vote, the president said, "They have shamed us in the eyes of the world."

Four weeks later, Wilson was awarded the Nobel Peace Prize. Josephus Daniels, the president's secretary of the navy, would write, "[Awarding Wilson the Nobel Peace Prize] was the court of world opinion overruling the act of the United States Senate."

The United States later signed separate peace treaties with Germany, Austria, and Hungary. The League of Nations was established, but America was not part of it. And, as Wilson had feared, without the influence and power of the United States it would ultimately fail.

As the 1920 presidential election approached, Democratic party leaders realized that Wilson was in no condition to run for a third term. The feeble president could not at first accept that reality, and those closest to him,

Edith, Grayson, and Tumulty, could not bear to tell him the truth. As preparations for the Democratic Convention began, he still harbored the hope and illusion that he might be nominated. But it was Ohio governor James Cox who received the nomination.

The Republicans nominated Warren G. Harding, one of the senators who had actively opposed the peace treaty. Harding promised a return to "normalcy." Apparently, this was what Americans—drained by war and weary of the postwar bickering in Congress—wanted. That mood, complicated by a broken incumbent who was unable to campaign for the Democratic nominee, led to a landslide victory for Harding. On March 4, 1921, Wilson rode to the Capitol with the new president for the inauguration ceremony. Woodrow and Edith then retired to the comfortable house they had purchased on S Street in Washington, D.C.

Wilson was seldom seen in public after he left office. However, when a crowd gathered outside his home on Armistice Day, November 11, 1923, he spoke briefly from the steps of his

The Wilson home on S Street in Washington, D.C. *(Library of Congress)*

In one of his last public appearances, Wilson addresses a small group of supporters from the front steps of his S Street home on Armistice Day, 1923. *(Library of Congress)*

home. So frail that his voice could barely be heard, the ex-president broke into sobs when he tried to pay tribute to the armed forces who had served him in WWI.

But for a brief moment his old fighting spirit overcame the effects of illness and age. Wilson did not mention the League of Nations or its foes by name; he did not need to. In a clear, carrying voice, he shared his abiding conviction that his plan for world peace would ultimately win out: "Just one word more. I cannot refrain from saying it. I am not one of those who have the least anxiety about the triumph of the principles I have stood for. I have seen fools resist Providence before. . . . That we shall prevail is as sure as that God reigns."

The last week in January 1924, Wilson suffered a "digestive upset." As the week progressed, his condition worsened, and Dr. Grayson was called back from a trip to attend him. Wilson declined rapidly, and on Friday, February 1, his children were notified that he was dying. A bulletin was released to the press stating, "Mr. Wilson has suddenly taken a decided turn for the worse and his condition [is] very serious."

Reporters began gathering outside the house. On Saturday they were joined by hundreds of Wilson admirers. The crowd kept an all-night vigil despite occasional cold rain showers. On Sunday, February 3, 1924, Dr. Grayson emerged from the house to announce, "Mr. Wilson died at eleven-fifteen this morning."

Edith Wilson planned two funeral services, one at the S Street house for family and friends and one in the Bethlehem Chapel of the Washington Cathedral. Both were private services. Edith issued the invitations. The president and members of the cabinet and of the Supreme Court, as well as ambassadors and heads of foreign governments, attended the solemn ceremony at the Cathedral. Henry Cabot Lodge did not.

Outside Washington Cathedral, people lined the streets, heads bowed, as the choir chanted the recessional hymn, "The strife is o'er, the battle done." It seemed a fitting close to the life of a man who had always fought for what he believed was right whatever the personal cost. He had obeyed the admonition of his Presbyterian faith to try to leave the world a better place than he had found it.

Wilson was not without flaws. He was a complicated man, often contradictory in his behavior, stubborn and unyielding. However, although the United States never became a part of the League of Nations, Wilson brought a new spirit to dealings between nations that still survives. That modern nations are from time to time capable of looking beyond their own national interests to what best serves humanity is part of his legacy.

Five years before his death, Wilson said, "I can predict with absolute certainty that within another generation there will be another world war if the nations of the world do not [negotiate] the method by which to prevent it." Tragically, as the world would learn in 1939, he was right. However, his vision of an organization in which nations would work together for world peace did not die with him. In 1945, the United Nations would rise from the ashes of Wilson's failed League of Nations.

# TIMELINE

| | |
|---|---|
| 1856 | Thomas Woodrow Wilson is born in Staunton, Virginia, December 28. |
| 1858 | Family moves to Augusta, Georgia. |
| 1870 | Family moves to Columbia, South Carolina. |
| 1873-1874 | Attends Davidson College. |
| 1875-1879 | Attends the College of New Jersey at Princeton (later Princeton University); receives B.A. degree. |
| 1879-1880 | Attends University of Virginia Law School. |
| 1882-1883 | Passes Georgia bar examination; practices law in Atlanta, Georgia. |
| 1883 | Meets and becomes engaged to Ellen Axson; enters Johns Hopkins University. |
| 1885 | *Congressional Government* published; marries Ellen Axson. |
| 1885-1888 | Associate professor at Bryn Mawr College. |
| 1886 | Daughter Margaret born; receives PhD in history and political science from Johns Hopkins University. |
| 1887 | Daughter Jessie born. |
| 1888 | Mother, Janet Woodrow Wilson, dies. |
| 1888-1890 | Teaches at Wesleyan University in Middletown, Connecticut. |

| | |
|---|---|
| 1889 | Daughter Eleanor born; publishes *The State.* |
| 1890-1902 | Professor of jurisprudence and political economy at Princeton University. |
| 1902-1910 | President of Princeton University. |
| 1903 | Father, Joseph Ruggles Wilson, dies. |
| 1910 | Elected governor of New Jersey; resigns from Princeton. |
| 1912 | Elected president of the United States. |
| 1914 | World War I begins in Europe; Ellen Wilson dies. |
| 1915 | Meets and marries Edith Bolling Galt; *Lusitania* sunk. |
| 1916 | Reelected president. |
| 1917 | Asks Congress to declare war on the Central Powers. |
| 1918 | World War I ends. |
| 1920 | Senate defeats the Treaty of Versailles; Nineteenth Amendment passed (women's suffrage); Wilson awarded Nobel Peace Prize; Warren G. Harding elected president. |
| 1924 | Wilson dies at his home and is buried in the crypt of the National Cathedral, Washington, D.C. |

# SOURCES

**CHAPTER ONE: Early Years**

p. 14, "Mr. Lincoln was elected . . ." Ray Stannard Baker, *Woodrow Wilson: Life and Letters,* vol. I (New York: Charles Scribner's Sons, 1946), 28.

p. 16, "I am a murderer . . ." Baker, *Woodrow Wilson*, vol. I, 44.

p. 17, "To save time is to . . ." August Heckscher, *Woodrow Wilson* (New York: Charles Scribner's Sons, Macmillan Publishing Company, 1991), 22.

p. 17, "I do not see . . ." Baker, *Woodrow Wilson*, vol. I, 68.

p. 18, "Tommy Wilson would be . . ." Ibid., 74.

p. 19, "seemed to be good . . ." Heckscher, *Woodrow Wilson,* 28.

p. 20, "magical years," Ibid., 36.

p. 20, "acquire knowledge that . . ." Baker, *Woodrow Wilson*, vol. I, 104.

p. 21, "Thomas Woodrow Wilson . . ." Ibid.

p. 22, "*Everything* depends upon . . ." Heckscher, *Woodrow Wilson*, 41.

**CHAPTER TWO: Finding a Path**

p. 23, "The profession I chose . . ." Eleanor Wilson McAdoo, ed., *The Priceless Gift: The Love Letters of Woodrow Wilson and Ellen Axson Wilson* (New York: McGraw-Hill Book Company, Inc., 1962), 31.

p. 23, "I wish . . . to record . . ." Baker, *Woodrow Wilson*, vol. I, 116.

p. 24, "full of fun and tomfoolery," Henry Wilkenson Bragdon, *Woodrow Wilson: The Academic Years* (Cambridge, MA: The Belknap Press of Harvard University Press, 1967), 72.

p. 24, "thou illimitable idiot," Arthur S. Link, ed., *The Papers of Woodrow Wilson,* vol. V of 69 (Princeton, NJ: Princeton University Press, 1968), 137.

p. 24, "a very jolly, amusing . . ." Bragdon, *Woodrow Wilson,* 72.

p. 25, "How can a man . . ." Baker, *Woodrow Wilson,* vol. I, 130.

p. 25, "The philosophical study . . ." Kendrick A. Clements, *Woodrow Wilson: World Statesman* (Boston: G. K. Hall & Co., 1987), 11.

p. 26, "My purpose in coming to the university . . ." Baker, *Woodrow Wilson,* vol. I, 172.

p. 28, "bright, pretty face . . ." McAdoo, *The Priceless Gift,* 4.

p. 28, "without knowing it . . ." Heckscher, *Woodrow Wilson,* 64.

p. 28, "I've made up . . ." Ibid.

p. 29, "I remember being . . ." McAdoo, *The Priceless Gift,* 12.

p. 29, "Professors could not . . ." Ibid., 32.

p. 29, "the occupancy of office . . ." Ibid.

p. 29, "*outside* force in politics," Ibid.

p. 29-30, "to contribute to our . . ." Ibid.

p. 30, "lurking sense of . . ." Ibid., 118.

p. 30, "I have no patience . . ." Ibid.

p. 31-32, "I suppose there never . . ." Ibid., 19.

p. 32, "I am at a loss to . . ." Ibid., 21.

p. 32, "Thoughts of you fill . . ." Ibid., 24.

p. 33, "Women . . . have mental . . ." Ibid., 123-24.

p. 33, "It hurts me . . . to think . . ." Ibid., 127.

p. 34, "I should certainly accept . . ." Ibid., 96.

p. 34, "I fear you would . . ." Ibid., 97.

p. 35, "They have actually . . ." Ibid., 98.

p. 35, "I have heard from . . ." Ibid., 108.

p. 35, "Won't you be thinking . . ." Ibid., 109.

p. 35, "*Can* it be true that . . ." Ibid., 113.

p. 36, "There surely never . . ." Ibid., 101.

p. 36, "longing to do immortal . . ." Baker, *Woodrow Wilson*, vol. I, 242.

## CHAPTER THREE: The Professor

p. 37, "I was desperately in need . . ." Bragdon, *Woodrow Wilson*, 146.

p. 38, "a *great* deal rather . . ." Clements, *Woodrow Wilson*, 17.

p. 39, "Ah, Sweetheart, it seemed . . ." Frances Wright Saunders, *Ellen Axson Wilson: First Lady Between Two Worlds* (Chapel Hill, NC: University of North Carolina Press, 1985), 68-69.

p. 39, "I *know* that no [little] . . ." Ibid., 69.

p. 39, *"My own precious little. . ."* McAdoo, *The Priceless Gift,* 157.

p. 40, "Lecturing to young . . ." Clements, *Woodrow Wilson*, 18.

p. 41, "The method of political . . ." Ibid., 20.

p. 41, "want with *eleven* rooms," Heckscher, *Woodrow Wilson*, 89.

p. 42, "Thirty-one years old . . ." Baker, *Woodrow Wilson*, vol. I, 289.

p. 42, "Her loss has left me . . ." Link, *Papers*, vol. V, 726.

p. 43, "I have for a long time . . ." Baker, *Woodrow Wilson*, vol. I, 295.

p. 43, "I can see him now . . ." Bragdon, *Woodrow Wilson*, 168.

p. 44, "the feeling that . . ." Saunders, *Ellen Axson Wilson,* 79.

## CHAPTER FOUR: Reaching the Emerald City

p. 48, "the perfect place . . ." David D. Anderson, *Woodrow Wilson* (Boston: Twayne Publishers, 1978), 58.

p. 50, "Here's to Woodrow Wilson . . ." Bragdon, *Woodrow Wilson*, 208.

p. 50, "Dr. Wilson is here . . ." Link, *Papers,* vol. VI, 88.

p. 50-51, "I need your advice . . ." McAdoo, *The Priceless Gift,* 177.

p. 52, "I find that I'm getting . . ." Ibid., 181.

p. 53, "Can we not persuade . . ." Heckscher, *Woodrow Wilson*, 121.

p. 54, "I am counting so . . ." McAdoo, *The Priceless Gift,* 202.

p. 54, "most promising patient," Heckscher, *Woodrow Wilson*, 121.

p. 54, "exhilarating beyond expression," Ibid., 122.

p. 55, "concerned with righteousness . . ." Clements, *Woodrow Wilson*, 26.

p. 55, "It was the most brilliant . . ." McAdoo, *The Priceless Gift,* 207.

p. 58, "in love with . . ." Heckscher, *Woodrow Wilson*, 122.

p. 58, "a devotee of pleasure," Ibid., 123.

p. 58, "Now comes something . . ." McAdoo, *The Priceless Gift,* 211.

p. 58, "no less than ten thousand . . ." Ibid., 221.

p. 59, "In planning for Princeton . . ." Arthur S. Link, *Wilson,* vol. I (Princeton, New Jersey: Princeton University Press, 1947), 38.

p. 59, "It has settled the future . . ." Ibid.

## CHAPTER FIVE: From Princeton to Politics

p. 60, "I feel like a new prime minister . . ." Anderson, *Woodrow Wilson,* 88.

p. 60, "that great, stately . . ." Ibid., 87.

p. 62, "informed and thoughtful men," Bragdon, *Woodrow Wilson,* 285.

p. 62, "critical," Heckscher, *Woodrow Wilson,* 138.

p. 63, "The importance of the . . ." Link, *Wilson,* vol. I, 41.

p. 63, "official beggar," Heckscher, *Woodrow Wilson,* 142.

p. 64, "place. . .where there are . . ." Ibid., 140.

p. 64, "I hope you will . . ." Ibid.

p. 64, "life-long friend and . . ." Ibid., 141.

p. 64, "second honeymoon," Link, *Papers,* vol. XIV, 422.

p. 66, "Princeton's most valuable . . ." Link, *Wilson,* vol. I, 44.

p. 67, "No doubt God *could* . . ." Link, *Papers,* vol. XVI, 451.

p. 67, "I have tramped as . . ." Ibid., 452.

p. 68, "I have every . . ." Ibid., 453.

p. 69, "I love my work . . ." Ibid.

p. 69, "academic communities," Link, *Wilson,* vol. I, 47.

p. 69, "We have tutor and . . ." Clements, W*oodrow Wilson,* 38.

p. 69-70, "Nations and all big . . ." McAdoo, *The Priceless Gift,* 243.

p. 70, "There is always the . . ." Ibid., 244.

p. 70, "so entirely admire . . ." Heckscher, *Woodrow Wilson,* 162.

p. 72, "a folly . . . loathed and . . ." Ibid., 355.

p. 72, "a great deal . . . your injunction," Saunders, *Ellen Axson Wilson,* 188.

p. 73, "You have only to . . ." Clements, *Woodrow Wilson,* 44.

p. 73, "We mean to build . . ." Bragdon, *Woodrow Wilson,* 286.

p. 74, "We have beaten the . . ." Heckscher, *Woodrow Wilson,* 200.

## CHAPTER SIX: The Journey Begins

p. 77, "I have always. . ." Clements, *Woodrow Wilson,* 54.

p. 77-78, "I am sure I can . . ." Ibid.

p. 78-79, "We suspected that . . ." John Braeman, ed., *Wilson* (Englewood Cliffs, NJ: Prentice-Hall. Inc., 1972), 97.

p. 79, "I shall enter upon . . ." David W. Hirst, *Woodrow Wilson, Reform Governor, A Documentary Narrative* (Princeton, NJ: D. Van Nostrand Company, Inc., 1965), 53, 57, 58.

p. 79, "the strongest candidate . . ." Link, *Wilson,* vol. I, 169.

p. 80, "The G.O.P. is in the soup!" Ibid., 171.

p. 81, "If elected, I shall . . ." Clements, *Woodrow Wilson,* 58.

p. 83, "I feel pretty confident . . ." Donald Day, ed., *Woodrow Wilson's Own Story* (Boston: Little, Brown and Company, 1952), 107.

p. 83, "All sorts . . . and spokesman," Heckscher, *Woodrow Wilson,* 219-20.

p. 85, "It is the people . . ." Clements, *Woodrow Wilson,* 62.

p. 86, "The present legislature . . ." Heckscher, *Woodrow Wilson,* 227.

p. 86, "nothing of substantial importance . . ." Ibid.

p. 86, "no campaign," Ibid., 238.

p. 86, "I am not to be . . ." Link, *Woodrow Wilson,* 314.

p. 87, "Isn't it all . . ." McAdoo, *The Priceless Gift,* 268.

p. 89, "Just between you . . ." Clements, *Woodrow Wilson,* 76.

p. 91, "Now we can . . ." Heckscher, *Woodrow Wilson,* 249.

p. 92, "You've passed him!" Link, *Papers,* vol. XXIV, 516.

p. 92, "Won't you please . . ." Ibid.

p. 92, "Governor Wilson received . . ." Ibid.

p. 93, "I cannot say to . . ." Heckscher, *Woodrow Wilson,* 243.

p. 93, "Of course I do not . . ." Baker, *Woodrow Wilson,* vol. II, 358.

P. 93, "Well, dear . . ." Saunders, *Ellen Axson Wilson,* 227.

## CHAPTER SEVEN: To the White House

p. 95, "The life I am . . ." Link, *Papers,* vol. XXIV, 551.

p. 98-99, "Once the government . . ." Link, *Papers,* vol. XXV, 73.

p. 99, "take care of the . . ." Kendrick A. Clements, *The Presidency of Woodrow Wilson* (Lawrence, KS: University Press of Kansas, 1992), 28.

p. 100, "For beauty I am . . ." Anderson, *Woodrow Wilson,* 105.

p. 100, "right out of my . . ." Heckscher, *Woodrow Wilson,* 258.

p. 100, "What I am interested . . ." Link, *Papers,* vol. XXV, 176.

p. 101, "a new freedom for America," Ibid., 327.

p. 102, "I shall have to . . ." Heckscher, *Woodrow Wilson,* 261.

p. 102, "He's elected, Mrs. Wilson," Saunders, *Ellen Axson Wilson,* 230.

p. 102, "My dear, I want to . . ." Ibid.

p. 103, "I have no feeling . . ." Link, *Papers,* vol. XXV, 520.

**CHAPTER EIGHT: Hour of Gold, Hour of Lead**

p. 104, "I find myself . . ." Ibid., 540.

p. 105, "exchanging confidences . . ." Heckscher, *Woodrow Wilson,* 239.

p. 105, "My dear Friend, we . . ." Ibid.

p. 105, "I can do my . . ." Ibid.

p. 106, "I have been . . ." Day, *Woodrow Wilson's Own Story,* 140.

p. 107, "let the people . . ." William Seale, *The President's House, A History,* vol. II (Washington, D.C.: White House Historical Association, 1986), 767.

p. 108, "We have built up . . ." Link, *Papers,* vol. XXVII, 149-50.

p. 111, "This is not a . . ." Ibid., 151-52.

p. 112, "I am going to . . ." John A. Garraty, *Woodrow Wilson* (New York: Harper and Row, Publishers, Inc., 1970), 78.

p. 112, "If you pursue this . . ." Ibid., 79.

p. 112, "I'll change that . . ." McAdoo, *The Priceless Gift,* 277.

p. 113, "The town is agog . . ." Link, *Papers,* vol. XXVII, 273.

p. 114, "a human being . . ." Ibid.

p. 114, "I cannot choose . . ." Heckscher, *Woodrow Wilson,* 308

p. 114, "It is very wonderful . . ." Ibid., 315.

p. 115-116, "A boy never gets . . ." Link, *Wilson,* vol. I, 3.

p. 116, "We have no sympathy . . ." Dumas Malone, ed.,

*Dictionary of American Biography,* vol. X of XX (New York: Charles Scribner's Sons, 1936), 357.

p. 118, "so far advanced . . ." Seale, *The President's House,* 788.

p. 118, "Oh, my God, what am I to do?" Heckscher, *Woodrow Wilson,* 335.

p. 118, "sobbed uncontrollably, " Ibid.

p. 119, "I do not see the light . . ." Louis Auchincloss, *Woodrow Wilson* (New York: Penguin Putnam Inc., 2000), 60.

p. 119, "We must be grateful . . ." Seale, *The President's House,* 791.

**CHAPTER NINE: Making the World Safe for Democracy**

p. 120, "in thought as . . ." Day, *Woodrow Wilson's Own Story,* 166.

p. 123, "It is amazing how . . ." Baker, *Woodrow Wilson,* vol. v, 139.

p. 124, "I cannot tell . . ." Ibid., 141.

p. 124, "It [was] the . . ." Seale, *The President's House,* 795.

p. 125, "About ten minutes," Ibid.

p. 125, "Oh, you can't love me . . ." Ibid.

p. 126, "You are so . . ." Heckscher, *Woodrow Wilson,* 351.

p. 127, "It seems the President . . ." Auchincloss, *Woodrow Wilson,* 62.

p. 127, "stained and unworthy . . . repented of," Heckscher, *Woodrow Wilson,* 355.

p. 127, "I will stand by you . . ." Ibid.

p. 127-128, "I remember those . . ." Seale, *The President's House,* 798.

p. 129, "He is a friend . . ." Heckscher, *Woodrow Wilson,* 397.

p. 131, "He kept us out . . ." Garraty, *Woodrow Wilson,* 108.

p. 131, "I can't keep the . . ." Ibid., 108-09.

p. 131, "They talk of me. . ." Ibid., 109.

p. 131, "a peace without . . ." Arthur S. Link, *Woodrow Wilson:*

*Revolution, War, and Peace* (Wheeling, IL: Harlan Davidson, Inc., 1979), 62.

p. 132, "would mean peace . . ." Ibid.

p. 133, "The world must be made. . ." Arthur S. Link, *Woodrow Wilson: A Brief Biography* (Cleveland, OH: The World Publishing Company, 1963), 113.

p. 133, "With a profound . . ." Arthur Walworth, *Woodrow Wilson,* 3rd ed., (New York: W. W. Norton & Company, Inc., 1978), 99.

p. 133, "for the privilege of . . ." Clements, *Woodrow Wilson, World Statesman,* 169.

p. 133-134, "To such a task . . ." Link, *A Brief Biography,* 113.

p. 134, "As head of a . . ." Link, *Woodrow Wilson: Revolution, War, and Peace,* 71.

**CHAPTER TEN: War**

p. 138, "meatless days . . ." David Jacobs, *An American Conscience: Woodrow Wilson's Search for World Peace* (New York: Harper & Row, Publishers, 1973), 94.

p. 138, "had no quarrel . . ." Heckscher, *Woodrow Wilson,* 440.

p. 138, "ridiculous and childish," Ibid., 450.

p. 138, "liberty cabbage," Garraty, *Woodrow Wilson,* 127.

p. 139, "detestable suffragettes," Phyllis Lee Levin, *Edith and Woodrow: The Wilson White House* (New York: Scribner, 2001), 180.

p. 139, "The women have . . ." Jacobs, *An American Conscience,* 94.

p. 140, "Just now there . . ." Heckscher, *Woodrow Wilson,* 468.

p. 145, "Force, Force to the . . ." Link, *Woodrow Wilson: Revolution, War, and Peace,* 85.

p. 146, "The Armistice . . . by example," Jacobs, *An American Conscience,* 103.

p. 146, "would certainly be . . ." Link, *Woodrow Wilson:*

*Revolution, War, and Peace,* 88.

p. 147, "The moment the President . . ." Heckscher, *Woodrow Wilson,* 490.

p. 147, "I believe . . . in Paris," Garraty, *Woodrow Wilson,* 138.

**CHAPTER ELEVEN: Peacemaker**

p. 148, "president of the World," Levin, *Edith and Woodrow,* 227.

p. 149, "life-giving to . . ." Ibid., 232.

p. 152, "We have assembled . . ." Jacobs, *An American Conscience,* 111.

p. 153, "a living thing . . ." Link, *Woodrow Wilson: Revolution, War, and Peace,* 99.

p. 153, "It was indeed a . . ." Heckscher, *Woodrow Wilson,* 536.

p. 155, "A group of men . . ." Margaret MacMillan, *Paris 1919: Six Months that Changed the World* (New York: Random House, 2001), 154.

p. 155, "a retention of . . ." Levin, *Edith and Woodrow,* 277.

p. 156, "looking ten years . . ." Heckscher, *Woodrow Wilson,* 545.

p. 156, "House has given . . ." Leon H. Canfield, *The Presidency of Woodrow Wilson: Prelude to a World in Crisis* (Rutherford, NJ: Fairleigh Dickinson University Press, 1966), 188.

p. 159, "Dare we reject it . . ." Levin, *Edith and Woodrow,* 308.

p. 160, "I promised our soldiers . . ." Walworth, *Woodrow Wilson,* 361.

p. 160, "There was nothing . . ." MacMillan, *Paris 1919,* 490.

p. 161, "suffering very . . ." Heckscher, *Woodrow Wilson,* 606.

p. 161, "The people . . ." Jacobs, *An American Conscience,* 149.

p. 161, "America is going . . ." Day, *Woodrow Wilson's Own Story,* 343.

p. 161, "There is one . . ." Heckscher, *Woodrow Wilson,* 609.

p. 162, "terribly sick," Jacobs, *An American Conscience,* 150.

p. 162, "It was the longest . . ." Heckscher, *Woodrow Wilson,* 609.

p. 162, "Nothing brings . . ." Link, *Woodrow Wilson: Revolution, War, and Peace,* 118.

## CHAPTER TWELVE: Journey's End

p. 165, "Woodrow Wilson was . . ." Ibid., 834.

p. 166, "We've been praying . . ." Heckscher, *Woodrow Wilson,* 622.

p. 166, "Which way, Senator?" Ibid.

p. 167, "Let Lodge compromise," Clements, *The Presidency of Woodrow Wilson,* 201.

p. 167, "They have shamed . . ." Garraty, *Woodrow Wilson,* 187.

p. 167, "[Awarding Wilson . . ." Josephus Daniels, *The Wilson Era: Years of War and After 1917-1923* (Chapel Hill: The University of North Carolina Press, 1946), 475.

p. 168, "normalcy," Heckscher, *Woodrow Wilson,* 637.

p. 170, "Just one word more . . ." Ibid., 670.

p. 170, "digestive upset," Ibid., 672.

p. 170, "Mr. Wilson has suddenly . . ." Ibid., 673.

p. 170, "Mr. Wilson died . . ." Gene Smith, *When the Cheering Stopped: The Last Years of Woodrow Wilson* (New York: William Morrow and Company, 1964), 244.

p. 171, "The strife is . . ." Heckscher, *Woodrow Wilson,* 675.

p. 171, "I can predict with . . ." Baker, *Woodrow Wilson,* vol. I, xvii.

# BIBLIOGRAPHY

Anderson, David D. *Woodrow Wilson.* Boston: Twayne Publishers, 1978.

Auchincloss, Louis. *Woodrow Wilson.* New York: Penguin
Putnam, Inc., 2000.

Baker, Ray Stannard. *Woodrow Wilson, Life and Letters.* 8 vols.
New York: Charles Scribner's Sons, 1946.

Bell, Herbert C. F. *Woodrow Wilson and the People.* Garden
City, NY: Doubleday & Company, 1945.

Blum, John M. *Woodrow Wilson and the Politics of Morality.*
Boston: Little, Brown, 1956.

Bragdon, Henry Wilkenson. *Woodrow Wilson: The Academic
Years.* Cambridge, MA: The Belknap Press of Harvard
University Press, 1967.

Canfield, Leon H. *The Presidency of Woodrow Wilson: Prelude
to a World in Crisis.* Rutherford, NJ: Fairleigh Dickinson
University Press, 1966.

Clements, Kendrick A. *Woodrow Wilson, World Statesman.*
Boston: G. K. Hall & Co., 1987.

————. *The Presidency of Woodrow Wilson.* Lawrence, KS:
University Press of Kansas, 1992.

Daniels, Josephus. *The Wilson Era: Years of War and After,
1917-1923.* Chapel Hill, N.C.: The University of North
Carolina Press, 1932.

Day, Donald, ed. *Woodrow Wilson's Own Story.* Boston:

Little, Brown and Company, 1952.

Dupuy, R. Ernest. *Five Days to War, April 2-6, 1917.* Harrisburg, PA: Stackpole Books, 1967.

Garraty, John A. *Woodrow Wilson.* New York: Harper and Row, Publishers, Inc., 1970.

Heckscher, August. *Woodrow Wilson.* New York: Charles Scribner's Sons, Macmillan Publishing Company, 1991.

Hirst, David W. *Woodrow Wilson, Reform Governor, A Documentary Narrative.* Princeton, NJ: Van Nostrand Company, Inc., 1965.

Jacobs, David. *An American Conscience: Woodrow Wilson's Search for World Peace.* New York: Harper & Row, Publishers, 1973.

Johnson, Gerald W., with the collaboration of the editors of *LOOK Magazine. Woodrow Wilson: The Unforgettable Figure Who Has Returned to Haunt Us.* New York: Harper & Brothers, 1944.

Levin, Phyllis Lee. *Edith and Woodrow: The Wilson White House.* New York: Scribner, 2001.

Link, Arthur S. ed. *The Papers of Woodrow Wilson.* 63 vols. Princeton, NJ: Princeton University Press, 1968.

———. *Wilson.* 5 vols. Princeton, NJ: Princeton University Press, 1947.

———. *Woodrow Wilson: A Brief Biography.* Cleveland, OH: The World Publishing Company, 1963.

———. *Woodrow Wilson: Revolution, War, and Peace.* Wheeling, IL: Harlan Davidson, Inc., 1979.

McAdoo, Eleanor Wilson, ed. *The Priceless Gift: The Love Letters of Woodrow Wilson and Ellen Axson Wilson.* New York: McGraw-Hill Book Company, Inc., 1962.

MacMillan, Margaret. *Paris 1919: Six Months that Changed the World.* New York: Random House, 2001.

Malone, Dumas, ed. *Dictionary of American Biography,* Vol.

10. New York: Charles Scribner's Sons, 1936.

Saunders, Francis Wright. *Ellen Axson Wilson: First Lady Between Two Worlds*. Chapel Hill, NC: University of North Carolina Press, 1985.

Schlesinger, Arthur M. Jr., ed. *The Coming to Power—Critical Presidential Elections in American History*. New York: Chelsea House Publishers, 1971.

Seale, William. *The President's House, A History*. Vol. 2. Washington, D.C.: White House Historical Association, 1986.

Smith, Gene. *When the Cheering Stopped: The Last Years of Woodrow Wilson*. New York: William Morrow and Company, 1964.

Tumulty, Joseph P. "Governor of New Jersey," in *Wilson*. Edited by John Braeman. Garden City, NY: Doubleday, Page & Company, 1921.

Walworth, Arthur. *Woodrow Wilson*. 3rd ed. New York: W. W. Norton & Company, Inc., 1978.

Wilson, Woodrow. *Congressional Government: A Study in American Politics*. Boston: Houghton Mifflin, 1885.

———. *The State: Elements of Historical and Practical Politics: A Sketch of Institutional History and Administration*. Boston: Heath, 1889.

———. *Division and Reunion, 1829-1889*. New York: Longmans, Green & Co., 1893.

———. *A History of the American People*, 5 vols. New York: Harper, 1902.

———. *Constitutional Government in the United States*. New York: Columbia University Press, 1908.

# WEB SITES

**http://ap.grolier.com**
Grolier Encyclopedia maintains a Web site devoted to American presidents, past and present.

**http://www.ipl.org/div/potus/wwilson.html**
The Internet Public Library's Woodrow Wilson page contains lots of information about the president, as well as links to other Wilson-related sites and online speeches and documents.

**http://www.whitehouse.gov/history/presidents/ww28.html**
The White House Wilson page has a brief biography of Wilson as well as information about the home of U.S. presidents and its occupants.

**http://www.woodrowwilson.org/**
Woodrow Wilson's birthplace in Staunton, Virginia, is now a museum, which also houses his presidential library.

**http://www.bbc.co.uk/history/war/wwone/index.shtml**
This comprehensive British Broadcasting Company site is devoted to World War I.

# INDEX